WINNIPEG

WITHDRAWN

WINNIPEG

D0442903

BEST JOB EVER

RETHINK YOUR CAREER,
REDEFINE RICH,
REVOLUTIONIZE YOUR LIFE

BEST JOB EVER

RETHINK YOUR CAREER, REDEFINE RICH, REVOLUTIONIZE YOUR LIFE

DR. C.K. BRAY

WILEY

This book is printed on acid-free paper.

Copyright © 2016 by C.K. Bray. All rights reserved

Published by John Wiley & Sons, Inc., Hoboken, New Jersey

Published simultaneously in Canada

No part of this publication may be reproduced, stored in a retrieval system, or transmitted in any form or by any means, electronic, mechanical, photocopying, recording, scanning, or otherwise, except as permitted under Section 107 or 108 of the 1976 United States Copyright Act, without either the prior written permission of the Publisher, or authorization through payment of the appropriate per-copy fee to the Copyright Clearance Center, 222 Rosewood Drive, Danvers, MA 01923, (978) 750-8400, fax (978) 646-8600, or on the web at www.copyright.com. Requests to the Publisher for permission should be addressed to the Permissions Department, John Wiley & Sons, Inc., 111 River Street, Hoboken, NJ 07030, (201) 748-6011, fax (201) 748-6008, or online at www.wiley.com/go/permissions.

Limit of Liability/Disclaimer of Warranty: While the publisher and author have used their best efforts in preparing this book, they make no representations or warranties with the respect to the accuracy or completeness of the contents of this book and specifically disclaim any implied warranties of merchantability or fitness for a particular purpose. No warranty may be created or extended by sales representatives or written sales materials. The advice and strategies contained herein may not be suitable for your situation. You should consult with a professional where appropriate. Neither the publisher nor the author shall be liable for damages arising herefrom.

For general information about our other products and services, please contact our Customer Care Department within the United States at (800) 762-2974, outside the United States at (317) 572-3993 or fax (317) 572-4002.

Wiley publishes in a variety of print and electronic formats and by print-on-demand. Some material included with standard print versions of this book may not be included in e-books or in print-on-demand. If this book refers to media such as a CD or DVD that is not included in the version you purchased, you may download this material at http://booksupport.wiley.com. For more information about Wiley products, visit www.wiley.com.

Library of Congress Cataloging-in-Publication Data is available:

ISBN 978-1-119-21231-7 (hardback)
ISBN 978-1-119-21233-1 (epdf)
ISBN 978-1-119-21232-4 (epub)

Cover Design: Jennifer Stott; Wiley
Cover Image: dem10/iStockphoto

Printed in the United States of America
10 9 8 7 6 5 4 3 2 1

Contents

Acknowledgments   *ix*

Introduction: My Story and Why You Need This Book   *xiii*

Chapter 1   You Don't Have to Wait for Your Dream   1
                 Career to Be Happy

Chapter 2   Eighty-Seven Percent of Employees Don't   11
                 Like Their Jobs: Here Are the Top Five
                 Reasons Why and What to Do About It

Chapter 3   Why You Haven't Changed Anything: 23
                 Career Fear

Chapter 4   What If I Don't Know What to Do?   37

Chapter 5   Career Excuses: All the Reasons You Don't   47
                 Have Your Best Job Ever!

Chapter 6   Career Boredom   53

Chapter 7   Redefine *Rich*   65

Chapter 8   Why You Are NOT Stuck in Your Career: 77
                 The Power of Change

Chapter 9   What Career and Life Do You Want and   85
                 Why?

Chapter 10   You Can Follow Your Passion Without   101
                 Quitting Your Job

Chapter 11   Career Plan Step #1: What Is Your Job?   113

Chapter 12   Career Plan Step #2: Discover Your   119
                 Strengths

Chapter 13   Career Plan Step #3: What Makes You   127
                 Awesome at Work?

Chapter 14   Career Plan Step #4: One-, Three-, and   133
                 Five-Year Plan

Chapter 15   Career Plan Step #5: The Big "Why?"   143

Chapter 16   Career Plan Step #6: Your Community   149

Chapter 17   Career Plan Step #7: Identify Both   159
                 Personal and Professional Barriers to Your
                 Success

Chapter 18   Career Plan Step #8: Achieving Your   169
                 Career Plan: The Power of Work

Chapter 19 Career Plan Step #9: Return on   177
Investment

Chapter 20 Career Change: Try Before You Buy   183

Chapter 21 Money, Finances, and Your Career Change 193

Chapter 22 When Everything Goes Wrong   201

Chapter 23 Start Doing: Take Focused, Smart Actions 211

Index   *219*

Acknowledgments

The Joy is in the Journey, Not the Destination

Writing this book was one of the most difficult yet most exciting things I have done in my professional life. Sharing the stories of my clients' careers–and of their incredible courage–has taken me down a very happy memory lane. I cannot thank enough, the individuals and companies I have worked with over the years. This book is a celebration of your collective career and life successes.

I owe an extraordinary debt to those who helped bring this book to life. I could not have done it alone and we all know it!

Thanks to my wife, Gale. I could not have done this without your support, your love, your "you can do this," and your courage. You are able to see me, my abilities, and my potential far beyond reality. Please don't ever see me as I really am! Thanks for giving me the quiet time to work, for reading chapters over and over again in the middle of the night so I could meet deadlines, and for never wavering when I needed a strong foundation to keep me standing.

Thank you to my children: Chloe (20), Olivia (18), Elle (14), Ava (11), Eve (6), and Crew (2). Chloe, your example of doing hard things and your weekly letters inspired me to write a book to inspire others. Olivia, the incredible music you played in the evenings sparked my creative mind. Thank you also for all your editing, suggestions, and help in creating each chapter. Elle, you always knew when I needed a good hug and a smiling face. Ava, your laughter helped when I felt like doing anything but laughing. Eve, thanks for your shining smile and going to bed on time so I could work. And last but not least, thanks to my only other man in the house–Crew. At two years old you caused mayhem and tried to distract me daily, but your infectious personality, smile, and laugh sure made it fun.

I have an incredible team. Thank you, Emily Socha, for keeping my business going even when I have run out of steam. You are invaluable to me and I am grateful for you everyday. And thank you, Jenn Stott, for being a miraculous graphic designer and making me famous for my slide decks, booklets, and everything else I need turned into "something cool." (Those are always my two-word instructions to Jenn.)

I have to thank my good friends who cheered me along the way. Brian and Julie Morgan, in the beginning, were more excited and took more interest in the book than even me. They also supplied me with an endless amount of soda to "keep me going." Thank you also to the following: Dave Wilkinson, who I have known since I was 13 and who still continues to talk to me at least three times a week; Justin Fuller, who is one of the smartest men around and the best "life and career" coach I know; Matt Christensen, a family-favorite dinner guest and the type of guy everyone should have as a friend who, when he decides to write his own book, will find it far more successful than mine; and David Burkus., who has already walked this path and provides invaluable insight and help as I begin this journey. You have all been so kind to help.

Thanks to my literary agent, Giles Anderson, who stayed so calm during the selling process when I was anything but! You helped get this book off the ground and I am very grateful.

I'm also grateful for my great team at Wiley. Richard Narramore, thanks for taking a chance on an unknown author. You have been fantastic to work with. Peter Knox and Tiffany Colon, thank you for bringing this book to life.

And thanks to YOU! Thank you for trusting me with your career I hope this book makes all the difference in your career and in your life.

Dr. C.K. Bray

Introduction: My Story and Why You Need This Book

Walking across the large stage as bright lights illuminated my path, I was only moments away from receiving my award. Considered to be a pinnacle point in my career, I had won the coveted top sales award and was being recognized in front of the entire sales division. Working for one of the largest companies in the world, I had proven myself to be one of their best; I was about to be presented the crystal vase and plaque to prove it. After accepting my award and returning to my table, I couldn't shake the feeling that the whole night didn't feel right, yet I couldn't understand why. This was a celebration of my monumental achievement—wasn't I supposed to feel like I had finally made it and was at the top of my career? But it didn't feel that way at all. Instead, I felt empty, worn out, and depressed. I could barely converse with the others at the dinner table as the realization poured over me that I felt hollow, unfulfilled, and miserable. I was in the wrong place. I needed to make a change. How ironic that the night of one of my greatest career achievements was the night everything started coming apart.

If I had only known …

Where It All Began

During the last semester of my undergraduate studies, I didn't have a job lined up. To be perfectly honest, I had no idea what I wanted to do with the rest of my life. What I did know was that I needed to find a job and I wanted to make money—preferably lots of it.

The majority of conversations with my graduating friends were about interviews and job offers: who of us had an offer and who didn't, who was in the final interview stages and who had been cut from the process. More and more of my friends were receiving written offer letters. Those letters were symbols that you were wanted and valued by corporate America. I remember standing on the doorstep of my friend's apartment while he read his offer letter. The high salary he was offered took my breath away. (Yes, I was jealous!) From my viewpoint as a poor college student, he had won the lottery. It didn't matter what the job was—he was going to make a nice, comfortable living.

So I began my own job search with only two non-negotiables. First, find a job in which I could make as much money as possible. Second, just plain find a job. Looking back, I am sad to note that I never (*ever*) considered the question: "Will I like the job I choose?"

At the time I graduated, one of the most coveted jobs was in pharmaceutical sales. If you worked for one of the big pharma giants, you were given a car, a great salary, and an expense account. I did everything within my power to obtain a pharmaceutical representative position, including stalking reps for job information and calling any district managers whose phone number I could find. After some hard work and lots of interviews, I convinced a very seasoned and successful district manager that I would be the best choice to fill an open sales position. (I did this by barraging him with hundreds of phone calls and voicemail messages reminding him why I was the best choice for the job.) Lucky for me, Woody Goodson gave me a chance, and thus began my career journey.

I started off with a bang. Woody was an amazing mentor. (The guy could sell anything to anyone—it was miraculous to watch him in action.) From him I learned the ins and outs of the business world: how to treat customers, how to interact with the vice presidents, and, most importantly, I learned how imperative it was to win. So that is what I did. I quickly learned that winning meant bigger bonuses, great award trips, and opportunities for promotions. My family was beginning to grow, and I knew that success would help me provide a better life for them.

But the newness and excitement of the job quickly wore off. A year into the job, I began to get a clear view of what this position meant for me. The actual job was not turning out like I had expected. Surprising to me at the time, the money didn't take away any of the sting of the dissatisfaction. I was beginning to question myself and wonder if this was what I wanted to do for the next 5 to 10 years of my life. During my long Texas drives in between customer visits, that voice inside my head kicked into gear telling me that I wasn't enjoying this. "But I am!" I would tell myself. I had a new company car that I didn't have to maintain, I was making great money, I had just bought a house, and I was starting to win some sales awards. I tried to tell myself that it didn't matter if I liked my job or not—I was successful! And so I silenced the warning voice.

So what did I do? In my great wisdom as a 20-something-year-old, I figured the best way to solve this problem was to get promoted and escape front-line sales. If I didn't have to sell anymore and I could be a manager, then I would like my daily work and that voice in my head would go away. So I was promoted and moved to Oklahoma. Problem solved, I thought. Fast forward another 18 months and I was promoted to work in New York. My work counterparts were excellent, we loved the neighbors, and found out in this position that I liked training and organizational development. But it still didn't feel right. So I got promoted to Texas. Loved my work counterparts, but still felt the same about the job. Got promoted back to Oklahoma. Same thing. Same thing. Same thing. You think I would have learned, but I didn't. Instead, my work life became more painful, and I was becoming more and more unhappy to the point at which it was bleeding over into my personal life.

In time, I changed from a normally happy, gregarious love-life type of guy to being stressed out and sad. I couldn't shake the black cloud that seemed to be always hanging over me and the work I was doing.

So I continued the battle against myself and simply refused to feel this way. I filled my time and occupied my mind with family, children's activities, hard work, church service, an MBA, working out, and triathlons. The more I sought to accomplish, the better I thought I would feel about myself and my work. Yet the moments would still come, those quiet moments when you actually let yourself think and feel. The raw emotion would occur late at night after my girls went to bed, or during a long drive when I would turn off the radio, or sitting in church, or watching work counterparts passionately discuss their weekly sales numbers. I saw that for many of the individuals I worked with this was their dream job and they actually had the life that I wanted: they had found a job they really enjoyed. They were happy and fulfilled with their work and their daily activities. But unfortunately for me, it wasn't the same. It was a great job for them, but the wrong job for me. (But how grateful I am now for that job and all the people I worked with over the years, because they took me down the path of discovering what I really wanted to do.)

Fast-forward 12 years, five moves, three different states, and four promotions and you find me sitting at the awards dinner wondering what I was going to do next. It was on that awards night that a painful realization came over me that I had sold out my dreams of who I wanted to be and what I wanted to accomplish for "things." Those things included the life, the house, the cars, and the image. I hardly recognized who I had become. I realized that no matter how hard I tried, how busy I had kept myself, I could never turn off that part of me that wanted to have a different job, one in which I would wake up in the morning and be excited about my work and feel like I was contributing to life in a productive way. If only I had known from the beginning the importance of having a career in which I felt a sense of meaning and purpose.

That evening began an incredible journey of finding my Best Job Ever!

The start of my journey began with deciding to work part-time and return to school to earn my first PhD in organizational leadership and development and later, my second PhD in industrial and organizational psychology. Near the end of my years of schooling, I began teaching at a local university, working with adults who were returning to school to earn their bachelor's degree. I worked with over 300 individuals weekly on career issues and organizational development. I am still close to many of my former students and credit them for being guinea pigs for many of my ideas and theories, systems, and programs regarding their career and personal development. They were such good sports!

I returned later to corporate America in a completely different role as a global organizational development and effectiveness vice president. (Try saying *that* three times without stuttering.) In this role, I was able to travel across the globe, working with individuals to develop their careers and their leadership skill sets. The international experience provided deep insight into how similar employees' needs are. Following a merger of the company, I started my own consulting business helping companies improve the effectiveness and productivity of their employees as well as helping the employees and managers develop their careers. This included providing them with training and tools to help them feel fulfilled and engaged.

It has been an incredible journey since that awards dinner.

After 20 years in corporate America, including education and experience in researching and studying careers, interviewing hundreds of employees and leaders, I am excited to share with you some of the principles I have learned and taught to thousands of others to help find greater success and greater satisfaction in their careers. More importantly, I have worked with and helped people just like you, who have struggled or are struggling with your own unique career issues and problems.

Over the last decade, I have helped men and women across the world to envision, plan, work toward, and obtain their Best Jobs Ever! By so doing, ironically and incredibly, this has ended up becoming *my* Best Job Ever!

Since most people are employed the majority of their lives, everyone should have access to this information on how to jumpstart their careers—to develop and create their own Best Job Ever! After years of hearing comments such as: "Dr. Bray! I have a friend who needs this information," or "I have a brother who wants to get promoted," or "My neighbor just lost his job and doesn't know what to do," I decided it was time to provide this essential career development information in a way that would make it available for everyone.

Whether you are searching for your first job, have been in the same career for decades, are returning to the workforce after a hiatus, are self-employed, or work for others, this book will help you discover and then work toward creating a career that will be most fulfilling for you.

This book:

- Is a step-by-step guide for anyone who is struggling with his or her career or for anyone who wants to avoid as many career obstacles as possible.
- Will provide principles, tips, questions to consider, and action items to move you forward in your own personal career journey.
- Will give you tools to help you discover what you want and steps to achieve it.
- Will help you in developing a meaningful career, whether that means making changes that will bring you greater satisfaction in your current career or helping you know how to get promoted or take a leap to another career.

If you read and implement what I am about to teach you, your life will never be the same. This process works. It has worked for hundreds of others.

The book is divided into three parts. Part One will help you understand why you may feel stuck in your career and how to overcome some of the obstacles to career happiness. Part Two will help you define your priorities to know what true success and *rich* means for you. It will help you figure out what you really want from a career.

In Part Three, we will discuss your motivation and create a personalized plan to achieve your promotion or job change or just help you get out of your career rut. I will share some of the principles that helped me be successful—principles that can help you be successful in your own career.

Your Best Job Ever! Rethink Your Career, Redefine Rich, and Revolutionize Your Life will help you identify and deliberately create the job that will bring you personal fulfillment and success. Hopefully, that will mean an increase in your pay as well!

BEST JOB EVER

RETHINK YOUR CAREER,
REDEFINE RICH,
REVOLUTIONIZE YOUR LIFE

CHAPTER

1

You Don't Have to Wait for Your Dream Career to Be Happy

The grass is always greener where you water it.

—Unknown

Success is liking what you do and liking how you do it.

—Maya Angelou

One of the first questions I ask my clients is, "If you could have any job, what would be your dream job, your perfect career?" Hearing their answers is always one of the best parts of my day. Let me share a few of their responses:

Client 1:   I would travel Europe for a year.
Me: That's not a job, that's a vacation. Try again.

Client 2:   I would own a business that I could live anywhere and
            only have to work three hours a day from a beach.
Me: Very few people I know can make a living working
            three hours a day from the beach to support their
            spouse and three kids with the same lifestyle they
            currently have. Plus you would get skin cancer.

Client 3:   I want any job that pays me double the salary I make
            right now.
Me: *Brilliant!* Except according to employee market
            values, you already make 15 percent more than you
            should right now.

Client 4:   I'm going to win the lottery so I don't have to answer
            your dumb questions.
Me: How long have you been playing the lottery?
Client: Twenty years.
Me: How much have you won?
Client: Fifty dollars.
Me: Excellent! You're on track to quit your job and start
            your perfect career when you are 2,500 years old.
            Why don't we start over and let's get you that dream
            job in the next year without the lottery. (This is where
            I restate my original question.)

Client 5:   Any job but the one I have now. It's bad, Dr. Bray.
Me: (Silence) and an "uh, oh" (This comment usually
            means an emotional breakdown is on its way in the
            next 30 seconds.)

Talking about your perfect career is difficult because it focuses on what you don't have now and everything that is going wrong with your current career. So let's take this in two steps. The first step is to debunk the myth of a perfect career. The second step is to discuss career happiness and fulfillment.

Your Dream Job May Not Be What You Expect

You may have an idea of what your perfect career looks like, but until you have worked that job for at least six months, you may be surprised that your perfect career is anything but perfect! More clients than I would care to count have come to me wanting to discuss their "perfect" careers.

"It wasn't what I thought it would be."

"It didn't give me the feeling I thought it would give me."

"I didn't make as much money as I had hoped I would make."

"I got bored of it so quickly, it didn't provide the challenge I thought it would."

"It turned out to be just as mundane as my previous job."

Do you notice some key words in their comments? It didn't give me the thought, feeling, money, challenge, or friendships I *thought* it would. Keyword being *thought*! It is hard to define a perfect dream job when you haven't worked at it for a significant period of time. Running a bed and breakfast along the beaches of Costa Rica may sound like a perfect job until you realize that you have to change sheets, clean toilets, and deal with grumpy sun-burned tourists every day. Not to mention you don't get to surf and paddleboard four hours a day like you *dreamed* you would. Doesn't sound like a dream career to me.

Another aspect of your perfect dream career is to realize that in most instances there isn't such a thing. The road to a perfect, fulfilling, and meaningful career is exactly that: a journey. I have learned from years of experience, education, and working with clients that your dream career isn't a final destination; it is a continuous road that you take throughout your life. As much as you and I would love to arrive at your dream career destination (as early in life as possible, please!) and set up shop for the next 20 to 30 years and enjoy job bliss, life doesn't work that way. Why not? Because your brain wants to continue to develop, progress, and take on new challenges, even if the rest of you want to remain in a steady state of no change. Once you have reached a goal, it quickly begins to lose its luster and you wonder what other things you might accomplish. Just ask Natalie, who landed her dream job three years ago.

It had been a while since I had worked with Natalie, so I was surprised when I received an email asking me for some time to discuss issues with her current position. I had worked with Natalie a few years earlier helping her find her "perfect" career, and in just under four months, she had done it! Natalie was promoted to her desired position and was headed to the West Coast. She was happy with her job promotion, as she enjoyed the organization she worked in, she made a good salary, and worked with dependable and competent people who liked their jobs. She found her job to be challenging and very rewarding. Sounds perfect, right? It was, except she was beginning to feel restless and ready for her next promotion, project, or "something different," as she put it.

After catching up with Natalie, she jumped right into what was bothering her. "I thought I had found my dream job. Now why can't I relax instead of looking for what is next?"

Natalie explained that when she got promoted to management and moved to her dream city on the West Coast, she thought this would be the last stop on her career journey. She had made it! This was the position she had always wanted, in a city that she loved, and now all she had to do was work hard, enjoy her great job, the warm weather, friends, and the beach. Except it didn't happen that way. ("Why can't life be more like the movies?")

The first two years on the job Natalie and her team won the top sales award and in year three she far surpassed her sales quota. During her management tenure, Natalie had promoted one of her team members, and because of restructuring, had hired and trained two other new employees. It was year four and Natalie's dream job was becoming not so dreamy anymore.

"I can't believe I am saying this, but I am not as excited about this position as I used to be. I feel like I can do more, and take on more responsibility. I have accomplished my goals. My team and I have won the top sales award, we have added some big accounts, and I find myself looking for what is next." She continued, "This isn't my dream job anymore. I can't imagine myself doing this for another 20 years. I would have to find another job. I need to find my *next* dream job!"

She couldn't have said it more perfectly! Many of my clients have experienced the feeling of attaining their dream job only to find that in a few years they were ready for something newer, more exciting, and more challenging. When you reach your dream job, you are going to discover that it is *exactly* that: a *dream* job—but only for a while! After you have experienced all that your current job has to offer, you may be surprised by what comes next. You are going to find yourself thinking of the next job and what the remaining years of your career have in store for you.

Other clients say similar things. "I am happy where I am and I have a great future ahead of me. I have no desire to change **but** …." It's the *but* that is the sure indication for me that everything is not okay. Their words may tell me they are content and happy short term, while their actions, feelings, and behaviors speak a-much different version of their long term career story. If you feel like I have just described you, hang on! I'm going to help you find your Best Job Ever through specific steps in the upcoming chapters. Get ready to begin your journey in creating your own every-evolving dream career.

The Secret to Your Dream Career

I hate to give away too much of the "secret sauce" at the beginning of this book, but your dream career has everything to do with your emotions, happiness, and daily state of mind and not only the job itself. You chase your dream job so you can experience the feelings that you expect the dream job to provide you; feelings that you are doing something worthwhile, that you are making a difference, and choosing your own destiny. Feelings that you are doing what you love while creating income for yourself and following your passion are a few of the descriptions individuals have shared with me when I ask what they want from their dream job. Those feelings and experiences are possible to have at any point in your career. *(Let me repeat that concept because it is so important.)* You can experience the feelings of your dream job by making choices today that create the feelings you are seeking. Some of these choices include learning how to progress in your career and deciding to develop your skills in areas that *you* choose. How you do your work and the influence you have on others are also important choices that create your dream career. These decisions and others can give you the dream job feeling right now. Let me share an example to illustrate the point.

I studied the lottery when I was a graduate student. Most individuals who play the lottery realize their chances of winning the million dollars is not likely to happen. In fact, the chances of winning the Powerball jackpot are around 175.2 million to 1.

You are more likely to be struck by lightning (1 in 3 million) or have conjoined twins (1 in 200,000) than you are to win the lottery. Yet millions continue to buy lottery tickets week after week. With such a losing proposition, why do people continue to spend their money against such odds? Two reasons: if the individual is lower-income, he or she may view the lottery as one of the few ways out of poverty (especially in a recession).

The second reason people buy lottery tickets is called a rescue fantasy, or, in other terms, the "feeling of being a winner." Yes, they are buying the feeling of having a million dollars. Every time they look at the lottery ticket, it sends messages to the brain to think about what they would do if they won the money. It is a brain party! And the party is all about the things and experiences they could purchase. When those individuals buy lottery tickets, they are paying for the thoughts and feelings of what it would be like to win.

The same goes for your career. You can create the feelings of a dream career right now by implementing the actions and decisions that will cause those feelings and experiences. You can buy that dream career feeling by the choices and actions you make today. And the result is going to be much better than an empty pocket like the guy who purchased the lottery ticket.

(Quick Note: if you have won the lottery, please email me and let's go to a steak dinner to discuss how I am wrong. Feel free to fly me on a private plane to meet you at some beach location and I will happily give you career and life advice at 40 times my normal rate. I promise I am worth it!)

You can choose to create the perfect career from the one you currently have by choosing to get promoted, or change departments, or you may need to step down and take an individual contributor role to get back in the game with a fresh, new start. You may need to change some aspect of your job or change aspects of yourself to create the dream career. You may decide to move to a different organization or start something on your own. No matter what direction you decide to go in, the secret to gaining the happiness you want from your dream career is in your hands. Let me share some career change examples in which some employees stayed in their same organizations while others chose to leave and pursue other options:

1. The corporate executive whose wife recently had a baby, who, soon after the new arrival, decides that being on the road, eating fancy steak dinners, and sleeping in hotel rooms are not for him anymore. His dream job is now one in which he doesn't travel as frequently so he can be home with his family.

   New dream job, same company

2. The lawyer whose dream job has turned into working 60 hours a week recently comes to the realization that she isn't happy. She does some research, talks to her contacts, and decides to become a professor and teach law school.

   New dream job, new company

3. The college grad who landed her dream job right before graduation and has now been in the workforce for the last two years. She wants a new experience, new friends, and a new city. She talks to her boss, chooses the promotion path wisely, prepares for interviews, and applies for a promotion. She gets the promotion and a transfer to the new city.

   New dream job, same company

4. The fast-food worker who is making minimum wage and is barely making it month to month. His dream job is

anywhere but *here!* So he bites the bullet, gets some financial assistance (it is out there!), and gets some training at the local technical college. Six months later, his salary has doubled and he is fixing refrigerators, washing machines, and dryers, on his own schedule.

New dream job, new company (his own!)

Recap:

1. Do not expect to have one perfect dream career. This is not a Hawaiian vacation where all of your focus is on just getting to the beach. It is a journey on which you will learn more about yourself and your dream career with each step that you take. View your current career as a means to discovering what is right for you *right now*, at this point in your life. (Even after going through the steps shared in the following chapters, nearly 85 percent of my clients have stayed at and found greater success and happiness in the organization where they originally worked. You may not have to look too far to achieve what you want.)

2. You can be happy right now in your career. Don't let your happiness depend on that one next thing you expect to happen. You can create a happy, fulfilled career now by choosing to create the aspects of your dream career you want, as well as developing yourself in ways that *you* choose. Much of your career happiness and fulfillment comes from the feeling of progressing in your career.

2

Eighty-Seven Percent of Employees Don't Like Their Jobs: Here Are the Top Five Reasons Why and What to Do About It

Oh, you dislike your job? Why didn't you say so? There's a support group for that. It's called, "Everybody."

—Drew Carey

I never get calls from clients on Friday afternoons because everyone loves their job when it hits 2:00 P.M. "How can you not love your job when you only have three hours left?" a client once told me. Thank goodness for Fridays! One of my clients described her exuberance of exiting her job on Fridays with, "I feel so alive when I walk out of the office on a Friday afternoon, I can't help raising my arms like I'm finishing a marathon." I laughed as I pictured her walking out of her office with both arms raised. She continued, "It's actually a marathon finish combined with a 'Hallelujah!' I made it through another week!" From her response, I pretty much concluded that she didn't really love her job.

You likely feel the same way; study after study tells me you don't like your job. Gallup[1] (2013) recently completed its State of the Global Workplace study and found that 87 percent of employees around the world are disengaged and don't like their job! This means that nearly nine out of ten people reading this book are likely to be unhappy in their work (or for those of you anticipating your first real job, it is likely you will be unhappy at some point in your career).

"Is it really that bad?" some friends asked me at dinner one night. "Why do so many people dislike their jobs?" That one question sparked a two-hour discussion that convinced me that I needed to include a chapter that was completely dedicated to why people dislike their jobs. While not the most fun, exciting, and motivating topic, it is important to identify what aspects of your job cause you to disengage from work. Throughout the book I'll provide ideas on how to find greater happiness and fulfillment in your career, but for now, we need to identify what aspects of your job may cause you to dislike it. In the words of my grandfather, "You can't fix a problem that you can't see or choose not to see." (He always told me this right before he told me what I was doing wrong.)

---

[1] Gallup, *State of the Global Workplace: Employee Engagement Insights for Business Leaders Worldwide*, 2013.

Let's take a look at what isn't working for you. It doesn't matter whether you work in corporate America, own a business, are employed in a small company, a recent college graduate, or re-entering the workforce after raising a family: this information applies to *everyone*. So let's open up Pandora's box and take a good, long look at the top five reasons why you may dislike your job and what you can do about it. It isn't going to be pretty, but what you find out about yourself and your career is going to be highly valuable and will help you make better decisions in the future.

The Top Five Reasons Why People Dislike Their Jobs

1. Bad Boss or Poor Management

"Never waste a good opportunity to learn from a bad boss."

If you or someone you know has recently quit his or her job, it is highly likely the boss may have been the reason. Employees have consistently stated that their boss was one of the top reasons they chose to leave an organization. "I quit my boss, not my job" is a statement I have heard more than a few times. The relationship between boss and employee can make or break a career as well as the success of the organization. I can think of managers in my career who have made a world of difference and one or two managers I wish I had never met. Managers who are successful have an ability to lead, inspire, and motivate their teams. On the other hand, ineffective managers can have a devastating effect both personally and professionally on the people they manage. A study conducted at the Hogan Institute asked employees to describe the top bad behaviors of their boss. I was fascinated by what they found. It's possible you have experienced a few of these behaviors firsthand.

The top bad behaviors of bosses include being:

Arrogant

Manipulative

Emotionally unstable and volatile

Micro-managing

Passive aggressive

Distrustful of others

Yet, as destructive as bad bosses can be, great bosses can make your work life fulfilling and enjoyable. They can turn a mediocre job into a fantastic career and make the culture of any organization a place you want to work. A great boss has a significant impact on your daily work life and how your career progresses. One of my own great bosses taught me a lesson I will never forget on how to treat the people with whom I work.

In my late twenties, our home caught fire while I was at work. My wife desperately tried to get a hold of me (this was before there were cell phones!). But I didn't arrive home until most of our house was a near-total loss. With a two-year-old and a newborn baby, the whole experience was almost more than my wife and I could handle. Having lost everything (yes, we only had the clothes on our backs) and now displaced from our home and living in an apartment, every day seemed like another mountain to climb. I had to continue working while handling endless phone calls with the insurance company and the contractors who were rebuilding our home; it was a nightmare. It was a dark time for our little family and one that still haunts me . . . .

Within a few days of the fire, my boss, Darryl, visited and delivered hundreds of dollars of donated baby supplies and another few hundred dollars in gift cards that he had collected for us. It was one of the most tender moments in my life to have another individual see the desperate situation we were in and do everything he could to make it better. It was a deeply touching time, and I knew by his actions he was a kind and good man who made a big difference at a vital time in my life. I have never forgotten what he did for us, and it has served as a reminder how I should always treat my employees. Darryl was known for demanding excellence at work, but he was also fair. Let's just say that I won him a sales award that year and produced more sales than anyone in that position before me. I did it because of the type of person he was, and he inspired me to do and be better by how he treated me. If you have a good boss, be sure to thank him or her tomorrow! If, on the other hand, you are dealing with a boss who might better be described as a demon than a human, keep reading for help!

2. Internal Politics

"I never repeat gossip, so listen carefully." —Old Joke

Internal politics are a part of life that everyone has to deal with. Different from organization to organization, the culture and leadership determine the types of internal politics that can occur. I can promise one thing: every company, whether large or small, is going to deal with the issue of office politics, and it isn't going away anytime soon.

You already know why you hate internal politics. Jack got the promotion over you because he golfs with your boss even though you are better qualified. You had better numbers last year, you worked harder, you took on more projects, you were more of a team player, you dressed better, and you don't have bad breath like Jack does. No matter the hundreds of reasons you feel you should have gotten the promotion, internal politics proved differently.

If you consistently experience office politics, you are more likely to dislike and disengage from your job, especially if you have ended up on the wrong end of the politics, like Susan did.

Susan was having a fantastic sales year. Her territory was looking to pass 150 percent of quota. Jan, a counterpart to Susan, was not having a great sales year and was hoping to skid by at 100 percent. Jan announced to her boss that after working with a new client for over six months, she had sold a large deal. Contracts were being signed in the next few days, and customer orders would be coming in soon. Jan was going to exceed her quota, and everyone was thrilled! Since Jan was now making her quota, the team was in contention to win an award trip, and life couldn't be better. Everyone was on cloud nine about the good news, until the first order was placed and Susan and Jan's manager realized the customer was not in Jan's territory, but Susan's. The customer sits on the border between the two territories, but after some investigation, the customer clearly belonged to Susan.

The politics begin as the decision has to be made who owns that customer. Should it be Jan, who has worked with them for six months and built a relationship, or should it be Susan, who really owns the customer because the company resides in her territory? What about the team award? How will that be affected? Let the demoralization, stress, and fighting begin! With office politics, there is always someone who feels he or she comes out on the losing side. This is bad for business, work engagement, and employee morale.

We hate politics in our business life because we want the work environment to be fair and equitable. We don't want to believe or perceive that important decisions that affect us are made on the basis of incorrect information and motives. If you consistently experience office politics, you are more likely to dislike and disengage from your job, especially if you have ended up on the losing side of a political battle.

3. You Are Overworked, Overwhelmed, and Undervalued

"When work feels overwhelming, just remember … it will end when you die."

You may dislike your job if you are overworked and overwhelmed. This is perhaps one of the most difficult reasons for many of my clients to come to terms with, because they, themselves, usually are partly to blame.

"But Dr. Bray, if I don't do it, no one will."

"My counterparts are so lazy, I have to make up for their incompetence."

"I'm working myself to death every day while Mr. Lazy is busy on Facebook doing the minimum and making the same salary that I am. It drives me crazy."

Sound familiar? While it may be easy to place blame on the company for the overwhelming amount of work you have to complete, you may have to share the blame. Outstanding, hardworking, and dedicated individuals like you can have a difficult time saying, "No!" An extra project needs to be done, "Sure, I will do it." That new employee needs to be trained, "I can help out!" you respond. We volunteer, say yes, or agree to things that we may not have the time (or the energy) to complete and then we go on to blame the organization when we are overworked and overwhelmed. Many of my clients have had to learn how to say, "No" to combat and fix the overworked and overwhelmed problem. Take a few days and evaluate your work to see if you may not be your own worst enemy when it comes to being overworked.

Feeling valued and important as an employee is critical to your success. If high-performing individuals are not valued, they may slip to become mediocre players. Remember, it is easier to keep high-performing employees at that level than to have their performance drop and have to spend time and energy coaching them back to excellence.

4. You Work with Not So Smart, Not So Hard-Working, and (can I say it?) ... Idiots

"Sometimes I sit quietly and wonder why I am not in a mental asylum. Then I look around at work and realize I may already be in one."

The importance of working with people you like cannot be overstated! Friendships at work can make up for and sometimes even prevent negative work issues. On the other hand, working with crazy people can cause stress, misery, and workdays that seem to last forever. You may dislike your job if the people you work with are unkind, mean, backstabbing, rude, gossipy, lazy, not funny, or loud breathers, and .... Should I stop there or continue?

Brett, a good friend of mine, found this to be true. He took a sales manager position that he felt was a good stepping-stone for his career. He had heard that the company was a good one, but also heard that some of the individuals he would be working with were difficult and sometimes downright mean. He decided he could handle the potential problems and took the position.

Brett quickly realized he had made a poor decision. It was a bad environment that soon began to take a toll on his health, his marriage, and his self-esteem. I encouraged him to quit and get out, but he felt stuck (see Chapter 8), as other positions were very limited in his small state. The focus of the leadership team soon turned on Brett, and he was demoted from his management position into a sales position.

As I watched Brett go through this experience, I saw firsthand the effect of working in a toxic environment and why employees will disengage from work if they are surrounded by idiotic people.

5. Your Salary

You can name your own salary here . . . . We just get to decide where the decimal point goes ($1,000,000 or $100,0000?).

You may *hate* your job (yes, notice I saved that word for pay-scale issues) if you feel like your pay does not match your work, effort, and time. The Gallup poll (2013) found that salary is one of the top measurements for why employees may not be engaged at work. Most of us feel that we should be paid more, regardless of our current salary. However, most companies are paying the industry average in compensating their employees. The question becomes who is right in the compensation battle. No matter who is right, the truth remains that employees will go the extra mile, be loyal, and do the right thing more often if they feel they are being fairly compensated.

Costco is a great example of this. They pay their workers 65 percent more than what Wal-Mart pays, which owns Costco's biggest competitor, Sam's Club. They also offer health benefits to part-time workers. These added financial perks have proven to be a benefit not only to Costco's employees, but also to Costco the company. Ready for this? Costco's employees generate nearly twice the sales and work of Sam's Club's employees. They also have a much lower turnover rate. The reduced cost of recruiting and training employees has saved Costco millions of dollars each year. Both employer and employee have won.

Now is your chance to consider how many of the top five reasons you are currently dealing with. Take a few minutes to think and write down the top reasons you may be disengaged from your job. You will need this information as you progress through the next chapters.

Top Reasons Why I Am Disengaged from My Job

1.

2.

3.

4.

5.

Recap:

Top Five Reasons Employees Don't Like Their Jobs

1. A bad boss—A bad boss is one of the top reasons that employees leave their positions. The future of your career and the success of the organization depend heavily on the leadership.

2. Internal politics—Internal politics are a part of every organization. While the politics may change according to the culture of the organization, it is important to understand how things work in your company.

3. You are overworked, overwhelmed, and undervalued— If the amount of work is disproportionate, employees can get discouraged and disengage from their work.

If high-performing individuals are not valued, they may slip to become mediocre players.

4. You work with idiotic individuals—Working with individuals who are self-serving, not collaborative, and generally mediocre can discourage high-performing employees.

5. Salary—Your pay has an impact on your happiness at work. If your compensation does not match your perceived effort and work level, you may dislike your job.

CHAPTER

3

Why You Haven't Changed Anything: Career Fear

There is only one thing that makes a dream impossible to achieve: the fear of failure.

—Paulo Coelho, *The Alchemist*

Courage is simply the willingness to be afraid and act anyway.

—Dr. Robert Anthony

I met Rob at a business meeting for entrepreneurs. He had worked as an accountant for 10 years until he couldn't do it any longer. He left to start his own business designing, creating, and selling watchstraps. On a break from the meeting, I asked Rob if he experienced fear when he left his finance career.

"Terrified" he said. "It took me much longer to leave than I originally planned. I had so many fears that everything would go wrong. It was a tough time in my life."

Rich, a good friend and extremely bright individual, wasn't accepted into his preferred medical residency program after finishing medical school. He was devastated. He confided in me that he didn't know what to do and felt like a failure. "I had so much fear that I wasted four years of my life and the thought of having to start over and figure out a new career was over-whelming. I have never been so worried. The fear of failure nearly killed me."

Amanda, a veteran sales rep, was up for a promotion. The interviews were to be the deciding factor, and interviewing wasn't her strong point. Amanda had a phenomenal sales record and won nearly every company award possible, yet she knew she needed to perform well in the interview. "I lose my train of thought easily and get all tongue-tied when I interview with executives," she shared with me. "I can't blow this, Dr. Bray. I am afraid that I am going to miss out on a great opportunity and not get promoted because of my fear of interviewing."

Fear!

We each experience different types of career fear. We fear we won't make our numbers, fear why the boss called us into her office, fear we won't get the performance rating or raise that we deserve, fear we'll fail on a key project, fear the customer won't buy, or fear we'll embarrass ourselves. One of the biggest fears is that we may get laid off or fired.

This one emotion has wreaked havoc in my life and career more times than I would like to admit. After years of working in corporate America and listening to hundreds of clients, I learned that I am not alone in dealing with this emotion. Looking back, I wish someone had taught me about fear and how to overcome it when I was a teenager. My career and life journey would have been much easier and a lot more fun if fear wasn't involved in so many aspects of my life.

How Fear Works

Fear is a dangerous companion when it comes to your career and personal life because it wants to ruin everything great you seek to accomplish. Fear will stop you from progressing, changing, and accomplishing. Here is how fear may work in your life:

- Fear seeks to rule the majority of your decisions.
- Fear takes no prisoners and is sympathetic to no one.
- Fear is a smooth talker. It knows exactly what to say and when to say it to destroy your courage.
- Fear is a master of telling lies mixed with a pinch of truth to divert you from the road you want to take.
- Fear's messages are never positive. Fear doesn't tell you to go knock 'em dead, that you can do this and you will be successful. No, fear is much more cunning and knows what you need to hear to persuade you to quit or at least slow down.
- Fear doesn't care about your age, your sex, your weight, your talents, your love life, or how much money you have. Fear doesn't care where you live, what you drive, how attractive you are, or your IQ. Fear does care about one thing—and one thing only: stopping you from progressing, changing, and accomplishing.

What Does Fear Tell You?

When you decide to start something that is out of your comfort zone, fear will tell you all the reasons you can't, shouldn't, and won't accomplish it. Fear's favorite "go-to" lines when talking to you include:

You can't do that. Don't you remember what happened the last time you tried?

You aren't smart enough, strong enough, skinny enough, cool enough, man (woman) enough, talented enough, or rich enough.

No one will help you. You will fail if you try to do it alone.

You are stuck where you are. You can never change or make things better.

You will never get promoted, so why try?

Don't do that! You will stand out and be different and people will talk, gossip, and laugh at you!

You don't have what it takes.

I am sure these sound pretty familiar. Here are a few more:

Fear lies to you at every turn, especially when it comes to the things you want most from your life. Fear will tell you to never chase your dream of returning to school and finishing that degree.

You don't have time, you don't have enough money, you will look like a fool, and everyone in class is much smarter than you!

When you decide to move ahead with courage and enroll in your first class, fear will quickly change its message and tell you

School won't be worth it. You won't get a new job or promotion after you graduate. What a waste of your time.

How You React to Fear

Spiders, heights, and speaking in public are just a few fears many face. But the fun really starts when we realize how we *react* to fear.

You might be surprised by your go-to fear response and reactions. Most individuals have one of three reactions to fearful situations.

The majority of people's first reaction to fear is to *run!* Immediately back away and run for the hills, get out, and get away. It's the same reaction you have when you feel something twitching on your leg and you look down to see a spider crawling up your thigh. You jump up, you scream, you swat it away, and then you run away. (Hopefully, not screaming!)

If fear doesn't cause you to run for cover, then you most likely fall into the second fear response category: you fight. For example, your boss stops by your office to tell you a customer called unhappy with how your project is progressing and she would like to talk to you in her office in 15 minutes. You get ready to go to war to defend yourself, all while expending massive amounts of energy through stress, anger, hostility, and defense mechanisms. When it comes to your career, this is one of the worst actions to take. It can destroy your career. Your caveman instincts of fight will not serve you well in most cases.

The third reaction to fear is to freeze. In the 1920s, Walter Cannon[1] first described the "fight or flight" response to a perceived harmful event, attack, or imminent danger. New research is taking this theory a step further to include fight, flight, or freeze responses. The freeze response is exactly that; you freeze, you can't think, you can't move, you can't take action, and you can't process information. This means when fear strikes, you do absolutely *nothing*!

You sit on the fence unable or unwilling to make a decision or move forward. This is the most dangerous of the three because this one can last the longest in duration. When you run away, at some point you will come back. When you decide to fight, it will

---

[1] W. B. Cannon, *Bodily Changes in Pain, Hunger, Fear and Rage* (New York: D. Appleton and Company, 1915).

come to an end once the problem or fear has been solved, but freezing can go on for days, months, and in many cases, years. I can't take your fear away, but I can teach you the steps on how to overcome it. (You can thank me later.)

How to Overcome Your Own Personal Career Fears

Step 1: Identify the Fears that Are Holding You Back. On the wall next to my desk is the saying, "What would you accomplish if you knew you could not fail?" I love that saying and wish I could live each day exuding that mantra in all my actions but, unfortunately, I have fear and lots of it. It seems that I jump over one fear hurdle to see another one 100 feet ahead. I have learned I can hurdle any fear as long as I can see it. That's what Step One is all about, identifying your specific fears and then writing them down.

I have a fear of success. I have sabotaged myself enough times in my life to realize that right when I get close to accomplishing something really great, I try to torpedo my success. Like the time I went to Lisa W.'s house in the tenth grade with some of my friends. She was so 1985 hot that when she asked me a question, I couldn't do anything but stare at her and mumble. I thought she would dig my caveman language and look past my 135-pound frame to see my incredible personality and wit. She didn't. Who needs enemies when we have ourselves?

Take a moment to identify your top five career fears. (Feel free to throw in your personal life fears as well if you are up to the challenge! Addressing personal fears will help revolutionize your life!) This is the first and most important step to overcoming fear, to identify it and bring it out into the light so you can see it is not as scary as you think.

Ask yourself:

What are you afraid of?
What is holding you back?
What are you afraid won't happen?
What are you afraid will happen?
What about your work keeps you up at night?

Your fears can be about any topic: work, personal life, your childhood, or anything else that you think might be holding you back. (Don't give me spiders or scorpions or snakes unless you work at a desert reserve. Heights don't count either unless you wash windows on a skyscraper.) I need you to focus on what is holding you back in this moment. Be 100 percent honest. You most likely don't even notice the fear because it has become your regular companion.

Step 1—Identify your top five career fears

1.
2.
3.
4.
5.

If you are having a hard time coming up with five fears, then try this experiment I conducted with one of my classes when I was a professor. While learning about fear, I asked my students to carry a three-by-five card for three days and make a mark on that card every time they felt some type of emotion that is connected with fear, such as anxiety, worry, anxiousness, and so on. Write down what specifically is causing this fear-related emotion. This assignment required my students to be aware of what they were feeling during the day. (Scary thought, isn't it?) The next day at 10:00 A.M. I received a text from a student who was vice president of a construction company saying, "I had no idea! I have eight fear marks and I haven't even gone to lunch yet. I was surprised at what I was fearful of."

Give yourself at least two days to discover what scares you the most. I have found that the fear of success and what comes with that success is more prevalent than the fear of absolute failure. It is more difficult for you to hide in the shadows when you are a success. What causes you fear? What specifically keeps you from progressing with your dreams? Talk to someone you trust and ask them if they notice any fears you have. Write those fears down and let them simmer in your mind for a day or two. Revisit them in a couple of days to confirm your initial thoughts.

Step 2: The Why of Fears.   Once you have identified what your fears are, it is important to understand *why* they are fears. You are afraid you will never get that job or promotion. Why? You think your boss likes Jane (and everyone else for that matter) better than you. You are afraid to apply for a job at that great organization. Why? You think they would never want *you*! You are afraid to go back to school. Why? You think you don't have the time, brains, or money. You are afraid to ask that person out on a date. Why? You think they would never like you because you have love handles and cankles. You are afraid to go to the gym, even though you have had that membership for two years. Why? You think it's painful to work out, you don't want to get sweaty, and you're afraid it won't help you lose weight.

Knowing the *why* of your fears will help you begin to take action to overcome them. I know this is not fun! Staring fear in the face is not a day at the beach. You need to trust that looking at your fear will help you move past them so you can begin to go after what you really want in life.

Step 2—Diagnose the why for each fear you identified

The Fear	The "Why" for that fear
1.	
2.	
3.	
4.	
5.	

Step 3: Even If You Can't Get Rid of Fear, You Sure Can Keep on Moving!   I have a new favorite word. *Despite.*

It keeps me going and often brings some wonderful endings to difficult and sticky situations. It's a word that I usually say to myself at least once a day and, depending on how the day is going, that number can drastically increase.

If used correctly, the word *despite* can be life-changing when it comes to feeling fear.

Jeff's story best describes the power of *despite.*

Jeff's career had taken a turn for the worse over the past six months. He was in trouble at work because his performance was down and his behavior had not proven to be much better. Jeff was feeling the heat. "I'm afraid I am going to get fired. What am I going to do?" he asked me in anguish. "I don't know if I can get another job that pays me near what my current salary is and I don't have much savings."

After listening, I knew we needed to discuss his options and plan how he was going to move forward.

But Jeff didn't want to talk about any of that; he wanted to roll around in his fear and misery a bit longer—and with all he was going through, I could hardly blame him. So I pulled out my favorite word and asked him: "What are you going to do about this work problem and what decisions are you going to make, 'despite' all that has happened to you and 'despite' whether it is your fault or not?"

He laughed at me.

"Despite?" he said.

"Yes, *despite*, meaning, 'without being affected by or in spite of.' So despite how you feel, despite how this is all unfair and might get you fired—what are you going to do in spite of what has happened?"

Jeff replied: "I never thought of it that way."

He realized for the first time that he had the power to change what was happening.

The same goes for you. When things are not going well in your life, pull out the big word, *despite*, and act accordingly.

Behave in productive, positive ways **despite** what your fears tell you.

Aren't treated well at work? Act kind and do your best, **despite** what others do. Dealing with discouragement on a daily basis and tired of the difficulties of work, life, and relationships? Act **despite** these feelings. This gives you control over your own life. It is quite liberating when you choose positive actions and behaviors over your fears and negative feelings. Too hard, you say? You only get good at this through practice, so you might as well start now.

Step 4: Look Fear in the Face (Schwarzenegger Style). Research study after research study has shown that facing your fears head on is one of the quickest, most efficient ways to overcome your fears. One of the reasons is that fear is often not based on rational thought. A study done in Australia took individuals who experienced hyper-anxiety and disgust when exposed to spiders.[2] (They called them *high-spider-fearfuls*—what a great name for participants!) They exposed half of the group to real spiders and half the group to life-like spider images and measured their heart rate and skin conductance. Then they switched the participants and repeated the same tests. The high-spider-fearfuls felt the same anxiety and increased heart rate looking at life-like spider images as they did at real spiders. There was no difference! In life, we often do the same thing; we become paralyzed by fears that aren't based in reality.

The study provided great insight into overcoming fear that you can put to use today! The researchers had the participants confront their fears by looking at the life-like spider images and holding the images in their hands. By so doing, it helped them lessen their fear of real spiders. Confronting your fears takes away its power so it loosens its hold on you.

One of the best things you can do is face your fear by placing your list of fears in a very conspicuous place that you will see every day. By putting your fears where you can look at and think about them every day, you will be amazed at how their power begins to disintegrate. Too embarrassed to put them where everyone can see them? Then hide them behind the mirror on your medicine cabinet and look at them every day while getting ready, or put them in a drawer in your desk and every time you open that drawer you'll be reminded of the fears. Try this for one week and see if it doesn't make a difference. You have to look and think

---

[2] A. Matthews, N. Naran, and K. C. Kirkby, "Symbolic Online Exposure for Spider Fear: Habituation of Fear, Disgust and Physiological Arousal and Predictors of Symptom Omprovement," *Journal of Behavior Therapy and Experimental Psychiatry* 47 (2015): 129–137. doi:10.1016/j.jbtep.2014.12.003

of each fear for at least 15 to 30 seconds daily to have maximum improvement. Take those fears out of the dark, look at them in the light, and watch them diminish in size as you realize that most of them are based in irrational thinking.

Conclusion

You can read every other chapter in this book, agree with what I say, decide to start making changes and move into action, but if you have not learned how to **recognize** and **handle** your fear you are dead in the water—doomed. I can promise you that fear will always be there (I speak from plenty of experience). It is learning how to move *forward despite* experiencing fear that makes the difference between paralysis and success. Remember, courage is merely fear that has been harnessed.

Recap:

1. We will all experience some type of career fear. No matter how your fear manifests itself, you must learn to identify, confront, and overcome it in order to continue on in your career development.
2. Fear will always tell you what you *can't* do. Learning to silence the voice of fear and continue forward will get you closer to the career you want.
3. Identifying which fears are holding you back is the most important step in moving forward. Don't skip this part of the career journey. It will serve you well later on.
4. Learning *why* you have your fears is the quickest way to silence them. Whether you are afraid to succeed or

fail, understanding the motivation behind your fears is crucial to continued success.

5. To overcome your fears, you have to look them in the face. Bring them out in the light, look at them, and you will see they are not as scary as you thought. If they still scare you, then return to identifying *why* they are holding you back. Dealing with those reasons will help you move forward.

CHAPTER

4

What If I Don't Know What to Do?

With Google I'm starting to burn out knowing the answer to everything. People in the year 2020 are going to be nostalgic for the sensation of feeling clueless.

—Douglas Coupland

One of my favorite things to do is watch people at amusement parks. Since most of my kids are at the "amusement park age," we seem to find ourselves at least once a year paying $100 a person to get into a theme park so I can buy $15 burgers and chicken nuggets. (Oh yeah—and we also go on a few rides.)

One hot and humid summer day, we were waiting in line for a ride that twisted every which way, flipped upside down, and then turned you back around again 20 times in three minutes.

37

As I watched the ride at full speed, I noticed a young man who couldn't have been more than 11 years old not looking like he was feeling so good. While everyone else was screaming and laughing with hands in the air, this young man had a somber face that was going whiter by the minute. Unfortunately, the ride had just begun and this boy was in for another two minutes of blender fun. I leaned over to my wife and kids, pointed to the boy, and told them to watch closely as this was not going to end well.

When his eyes started to bulge, I knew the ride was going to change drastically for his friends who were sitting in the same seat. As the ride began to come to an end, I was amazed at how well the boy held it together. It looked like he was going to make it off the ride before sharing his lunch with everyone. Unfortunately, I was wrong, he didn't make it more than five steps off the ride when he lost his lunch.

I wish you could have heard the gasps, screams, and moans that came from the crowd as people waiting in line watched the event unfold. The poor boy was going to be scarred for life because of this public humiliation. Just as I was hoping he would disappear into the crowd as quickly as possible, I heard a woman shrieking at the top of her lungs, "What were you thinking?" "Why didn't you do something?" All eyes in the crowd turned to the boy's mom as we watched her reprimand him.

I have never forgotten his answer, "I didn't know what to do. I was stuck on the ride. I just didn't know what to do."

Coincidentally, I hear that exact same comment in one form or another a few times a week from clients and workshop attendees, and in emails from listeners of the Career Revolution Podcast.

"I don't know what to do."

"I don't know what steps I should take."

"If I knew what to do, I would do it."

The look clients give me as they speak those words is the same look of desperation that I saw in the little boy's eyes on that ride. Employees are lost as to what steps they should take next in their career. They have a desire to find a job they like and can progress in, a job that provides meaningful and fulfilling work, while at the same time making enough money to support themselves and their loved ones.

As humans, we are wired to want to continually develop and progress in our lives, but that can be extremely difficult when you don't know what steps to take to reach your desired destination. This feeling of uncertainty can cause you to become overwhelmed and incapacitated, making your career (and life) journey feel like a never-ending amusement park ride in which unable to exit you become more and more sick.

To overcome the "I don't know what to do" problem of career development, you need to take three specific steps. They are simple steps but they are going to require some work on your part.

You are going to have to take time to reflect on your current situation and then take action steps to figure out what is the right job or career for you. You will need to uncover what you really want from your career, which is much harder than it initially sounds. When I asked you to write down five things (in Chapter 2) you don't like about your job, you were probably able to spout the answers off in less than 10 seconds. When I now ask what five aspects of your job you love, you will likely have a much harder time. It is human nature to have a clear understanding of what we *don't* like, but most of us have only a vague idea of what we *do* like. Thus, the reason for the following three steps is to help you understand what actions you need to take to further your career.

Step One: You Need More Information

If you don't know how to proceed with your career and life, you are lacking information. Your current view of jobs is most likely a limited one seen from the ground level. We need to expand that understanding to a more extensive and exhaustive view.

The problem often isn't that you don't know what to do, it is that you don't know what is out there. In many cases, clients don't even know what jobs are available at their very own companies, let alone all the positions in their city or state. There are hundreds of thousands of jobs out there, jobs that you don't even know exist. Companies are being started daily that could be the perfect intersection of your strengths, your abilities, and your salary needs. One Fortune 100 organization I consult with recently opened up a whole new division focused on innovation and new products. Companies and jobs are in a state of constant change. The job search you conducted three years ago is going to look much different from what it would today. I am *not* saying you need to look for jobs. I am saying you need to look *at* jobs. There is a big difference between the two. Getting a good idea of everything that is available both in your organization and at other companies can be vital to your career success. What are the different organizations looking for? What are the job responsibilities and expectations? Additional information will give you a good head start in figuring out your next step.

It is time to pull out your inner Sherlock Holmes to get the information you need, I highly recommend you spend at least two to three hours a week for one month looking at jobs. Visit the big job boards, check out career lists, and look at career blogs. Even take a look at your local newspaper's help wanted section.

I suggest you use this investigative strategy: First, look up every job that is similar to yours; same title, same market segment, same everything! Get an idea of how your job can look very different in other organizations. What are the requirements of your job in other markets? Is the pay similar? Do you have the necessary skills that are required? These are all questions you need to ask so you are aware of how your job may be changing with technology and the economy.

Next, search out your job title in different market segments. If you are a director of marketing in the healthcare segment, search out only the keyword *director*. You may find that your skill sets and competencies match that of a director of products in finance. Numerous job skills are transferrable to other market segments. You don't know what you don't know until you spend time researching what careers are out there. You have no idea of what may be available to you, including in your current organization. If you spend at least 12 to 15 hours this month searching jobs, you will be amazed at the long list of possible opportunities that are available. I can promise you will find areas that are of specific interest to you. The information you discover will provide great direction toward your next step.

(Helpful Hint: I encourage everyone, yes everyone, whether you love your job ... or not ... to spend at least two to three hours a month looking at job boards related to your specific career. More times than I care to count I have worked with an individual who has been fired or laid off and learned a bit too late that their competencies and skill sets were out of date. Keep current on industry expectations for your specific job. You may find that you need to update your knowledge in a few areas. It is better to know now than to find out later.)

Step Two: You Don't Know What You Like to Do

Getting a job that matches your skill sets, your competencies, and your personality with a great boss and counterparts can be difficult to find. (And don't forget you also want a good salary!)

The process becomes especially difficult when you have no idea of what you like, what your strengths are, and what job is a good fit for you. Here are some practical suggestions to discovering what you like.

1. Take the Strengths Test 2.0 by Tom Rath. (See resources on my website DrCKBray.com.) While this is not a specific job assessment, it will provide you with insight into your strengths and specific areas in which you excel. It is inexpensive and the information is well worth the price. Warning: I would avoid assessments that promise to match you with your dream job or the "right" job for you. There are some inherent problems with these assessments, one of which is the database of prospective jobs is not comprehensive. Technology and a global business environment are changing too rapidly for an assessment to provide you with all the information you need.)

2. Follow the bread crumbs. Finding what you like is a process and not an end destination. As you search out careers that interest you, find individuals who already work in that industry. Connect with them on LinkedIn or through other social media and see if you can talk with them or email a few questions on the reality of the job. What does a "day in the life" look like? Those individuals can give you a realistic view of the position, both the positives and the negatives, and also provide suggestions on other similar jobs. Don't make the mistake of jumping to another job in your organization or going to another company until you have done your research and due diligence. One "bread crumb" will lead to another as they begin to connect and show the direction that you should go.

3. Take a personality test. It doesn't matter whether it is the MBTI or the DISC profile. (See my resource page for the link DrCkBray.com.) You need information on whether or not you are an introvert, extrovert, or ambivert (that's a little bit of both and yes, that is an actual term used in research!). You need to know if your brain is more analytical or if you prefer seeing the bigger picture at work. Personality tests give you information on the *way* you like to work, not necessarily *what* type of work you would prefer. This knowledge will help as you are perusing jobs and their requirements, so you can better match the job to your strengths and also your personality.

For example, I am a very social guy. I like to talk to everyone and find out what is going on in their lives. I like to discuss projects, upcoming work, news, politics, sports, and the list goes on. If I work in an office, I tend to float around and talk (bother) everyone. I don't get much done (although I have more friends that way). But if I work from home, where the environment is quiet and I don't have access to people, my social side takes a breather and I am able to focus on work. I understand according to my personality and my strengths that I am more productive and I work better when I work from home. Understanding *how* you work is key to finding a good job fit.

Helpful Hint: Be wise. As you research positions and find areas of interest, be sure to take a moment to ensure that this is a viable job and there is a demand for the position (as well as compensation that is in alignment with the job). As great as any job may look, if there is no demand for that position or the salary is low, there is a *reason*! Back away for a time and think about it. Remember that there are plenty of good jobs out there (no matter what the news tells you) and you may need to continue your search.

Step Three: Make a Choice and Take Action

Making the switch from learning and researching to taking action can be difficult.

Researching and looking are fun! You get to peek through the window of opportunity and possibilities. The hard part is actually choosing and taking action (more to come on this in Chapter 23: Taking Action).

This is the point in career development in which lots of people freeze (because of fear) and get stuck. You begin to wonder if you are making a wise choice, and if it is really worth it to change. If you have done your homework, figured out your skills, strengths, and personality and have spoken with as many individuals as you can, then go ahead and choose the best option! If the path you are taking doesn't work out, then all you have to do is choose again! (Yes, you can continue to choose! This is not a one-time thing.) Career development is a constant progression of developing your skills and your talents and finding a match with the right job. It has taken me two or three jumps to get to where I wanted to be, but I learned necessary skills along the way that helped get me where I am now. I wouldn't be in this position if I hadn't worked at those other organizations. Moving from researching to taking action is a big step, but if done in the right way, with the right amount of preparation, the process won't be nearly as difficult or as stressful as it may now seem. In Part Three of this book, we dive heavily into the action steps you need to take once you have made a decision.

Recap:

1. As humans, we are wired to want to continue to develop and progress in our lives, but it can be extremely difficult to do when you don't know what steps to take next to reach your desired destination.

2. If you don't know what to do with your career and life, you are lacking information. Research the possibilities.

3. Identify your strengths and your personality type. This will help you understand the way you work best.

4. Gathering information is exactly what you need to do to help you make the best decision. Be careful not to get caught up in this step. The time will come when you need to make a decision and take action.

5

Career Excuses: All the Reasons You Don't Have Your Best Job Ever!

He that is good for making excuses is seldom good for anything else.
—Benjamin Franklin

I can't
I won't be able to
I wish I could
    But it just isn't possible
Because …
    So I could never

Because …

I don't have the right education

I don't have the right network or connections

I have kids, a spouse, and a mortgage

I am too old

I am too fat

I'm not smart enough

I don't have enough time

It's too late for me

I don't have enough money

I don't want to fail

It won't work

I need more time to plan

I'm too good looking … ***What?***

(Yes, I did have a client who told me he didn't get promotions because he was too good looking. He explained that his dashing looks made others feel insecure about themselves and he could see why they wouldn't want to be around him. That is why he was never promoted. I was so dumbfounded I could do nothing but agree with him.)

"*But*, I Have Good Reasons for Excuses."

Excuses are nothing more than rationalizations we tell ourselves about ourselves, others, events, and circumstances. It lets us pass the responsibility off and disperse the blame to anyone other than ourselves.

Why Do We Make Excuses?

There are as many excuses as there are people. Yet, I have discovered there are really eight reasons *why* we make excuses.

1. We are afraid we are going to fail.
2. We are afraid we will look dumb or get embarrassed.
3. We are afraid of change.
4. We don't like change, uncertainty, and not knowing what is going to happen.
5. We don't like to make mistakes.
6. We don't want to get in trouble or be blamed.
7. We don't want to look like we don't have the resources, the self-esteem, and confidence that others seem to have.
8. We are afraid of success and what that success might require and bring into our lives.

Psychologists put excuse-making into the "self-handicapping" category of human performance and motivation. It prohibits your ability to be successful. If nothing is ever your fault, how can you ever have the power to change what you believe is out of your control?

What Happens When We Make Excuses?

When you make excuses, you destroy your ability to move closer to achieving your goals and aspirations. Excuses provide you the reason to give up. The moment something gets hard, or scary, or you feel you might fail, you can just pick up the excuse weapon and have your means of an exit. You tell life and those around you that you have **no** intention of living up to your full potential. You are more than happy with mediocrity.

Excuses let you run away from opportunities and accomplishing what you may actually want out of life. The more you use excuses, the stronger the tendency to take the excuse route the next time something difficult rolls around. Excuses are a way of avoiding responsibility, avoiding work, and sometimes even avoiding success and all you might be capable of accomplishing.

But … I'm too …

Often when I hear myself giving an excuse or complaining, I think of Kerri Strug.

It was the summer Olympics of 1996 in Atlanta, Georgia. I was riveted to the television. The U.S. women's gymnastics team had never (*ever*) won an Olympic team gold medal before. The favorites, the Russians and the Romanians, were teams with more experience, more world titles, and big expectations to win.

The U.S. women's gymnastics team historically always stayed in the Olympic village so they could meet other athletes, watch events, and enjoy the whole experience of the games. Except in 1996 they didn't. Amid all the distraction of the games they decided to live in a top-secret location. The secret location was later disclosed as a fraternity house at Emory University. (Really? We want to make sure they are ready for the biggest sporting event of the last four years and we put them in a fraternity house? No one thought of or suggested the Ritz Carlton?)

The competition was fierce from the beginning as Russia led after the compulsory rounds, but the competition heated up after the United States pulled into the lead during each of the separate events. With just one event left, the vault, the United States was in first place with a strong lead. With the gold seemingly locked down for the United States, the unexpected happened, as Dominique Moceanu, the team leader and favorite, falls twice on the vault and puts the gold medal back on the table for any of the top three teams to win.

Next on the vault for the United States is Kerri Strug, who according to experts did not possess the competitiveness, the fire, or the toughness that many of the other gymnasts on the team seemed to exhibit. Standing tall at 4-feet, 9-inches, this Tucson, Arizona, gymnast was not considered a leader on the team.

In front of 32,000 spectators, Strug set up for the vault and then sprinted down the launch pad, hit the vault, spun one and a half times in the air, and made a blind landing. Kerri slipped on the landing and felt a snap in her left ankle. She immediately fell to the ground in pain. Unable to determine if this score would win the United States the gold, her coach asked Kerri to complete a second vault. She hobbled back to the vault line as the crowd jumped to its feet while screaming and applauding her bravery. "Please, God, help me make this vault," she said to herself as she waited for permission from the judges to start her vault. "I know I can do it one more time, injured ankle or not!"

Breathing deeply, she sprinted down the runway as every eye in the Georgia Dome was on her. Kerri came down hard on both her feet and heard a second snap in her left ankle. Holding the famous gymnast pose long enough for the judges, Kerri then fell to the floor holding her leg as the crowd went wild. As she was leaving the floor, the scoreboard flashed up a 9.72, and the United States women's gymnastics team won the gold! Everyone around the world witnessed an amazing act of courage and the event became one of the greatest moments of sports history.[1]

What made it even more memorable and cemented her status as a legend among athletes was the way she handled the moment. She chose to keep going and do the hard thing with no excuses, which is a lesson we can all learn.

However, the deeper and more profound lesson is that Kerri's decision to do hard things, not complain, and not make excuses was made years ago. It was made as she trained, day after day, coming in early when she was tired, staying late when she would have preferred to hang out with her friends and eat McDonald's fries, and go to a movie. Kerri Strug made that

[1] Rick Weinberg, "Kerri Strug Fights Off Pain, Helps U.S. Win Gold," www.ESPN.com, July 19, 2004.

decision over and over again all those years while she trained to become an international athlete. She exemplified a rare success-producing trait, the ability to do hard things and not complain or give excuses.

On the other hand, consider whether it was wise for Kerri to vault a second time when she was injured. Was it worth risking her chance to compete in the individual rounds? I love the lesson that Kerri taught us about continuing on when our career and lives become difficult, but it is also wise to know when to stop and cut our losses. Continuing on a path or in an environment that is not healthy for us can be destructive and have heavy consequences. The takeaway is to recognize when you are using excuses and not giving your best and then to determine to follow Kerri's example of excellence. At the right time in your life, you may be given the chance to have your own Kerri Strug moment.

Recap:

1. Excuses are nothing more than rationalizations that we tell ourselves others, events, and circumstances. We make excuses because we are afraid or want to avoid things.

2. Psychologists put excuse-making into the "self-handicapping" category of human performance and motivation. Using excuses prohibits your ability to be successful.

3. When you make excuses, you destroy your ability to move closer to achieving your goals and aspirations. Excuses provide you the reason to give up.

6

Career Boredom

Sometimes the best part of my job is that my chair swivels.

—Unknown

Dan always fell asleep during meetings. I loved to watch the process unfold, which usually began around 2:30 in the afternoon. His eyes would begin to blink, then the blinking became extended blinking (at least one minute in between blinks) and within five minutes his head would start bobbing. The head bobbing was always my favorite, as he fought a losing battle to stay awake. Come to think of it, I don't think he ever won. When Dan hit full REM sleep, his head would rest on his shoulder or chest and we knew Dan was out for the count. No one ever woke him up—meetings always went better if he was silent and we didn't have to hear his comments. Dan was obviously bored.

But who am I to make fun of Dan? I have been bored at work and spaced off to happier places more times than I can count. This is normal behavior for most of us as our bodies experience different levels of energy throughout the day as we engage in tasks that range from exciting to completely mind numbing. But when we talk about Career Boredom, we are describing a much different animal.

Career boredom doesn't stem from never-ending, pointless meetings, to-do lists that will never get completed, or from fellow employees who have the personality of a British security guard. (I mean the silent guards at Buckingham Palace, not the yappy ones you see at the museums.) Your career boredom originates from a lack of personal purpose, meaning, and motivation about your career. Some of the symptoms of career boredom may include discontent, lack of interest, sadness, or numbness (like when something great happens at work and you feel no joy or happiness from it). It may also include feelings of unrest and anxiety, or you may find yourself getting mad over minor things that didn't go well at work. Your health may be declining or you may not sleep well at night. You may experience depression or find yourself spacing off during the day. You may feel antsy or anxious without knowing why. (Five Monster Energy drinks don't account for the antsy or anxious feeling and are definitely not the best way to combat career boredom.)

Let me throw in a few more symptoms for good measure (in case you are a career illness hypochondriac): lack of hobbies, few friendships, weight gain, and anxiety. All of these symptoms can be caused by a number of different things, but they have also been shown in study after study to have a direct correlation to your J-O-B. Some of most frequent statements clients have shared with me in regard to career boredom include:

- I am overqualified.
- The work is boring.
- I have done this job for waaaaayyyyyy too long and it has lost its challenge and excitement.
- I mastered my job responsibilities long ago.
- The work I do is so boring. They have me working on the worst projects!
- The people at work are boring. Who needs to watch *"The Walking Dead?"* Just visit me at work.
- I don't get the same "high or excited" feeling from my work like I used to.

Every job—and I mean pretty much *every* job—has pointless meetings, employees who are less than intelligent (you know who they are!), assignments and projects that seem to have no purpose, or conference calls that are more boring than watching your local city council meeting on cable. There are parts of every job that are no fun, no matter what the industry. Yet, in spite of those boring aspects of a job, a person who is engaged in his or her job and feels it has meaning and purpose doesn't suffer from the negative feelings discussed here. When you know you have helped a client in a way that no one else can or you make a difference on a project, you don't experience career boredom.

Stephen Vodanovich, a professor from the University of West Florida, has studied boredom for 20 years and found that "people who are more likely to become bored do not see their environments as very lively or rich in meaning." Career boredom means there is little to no personal meaning in your job and no purpose to your daily work. The 8 to 10 hours you spend at work every day can leave you feeling exhausted, drained, and plain worn out. A whole new type of daily torture! This is a sad statement if you perceive your career this way. No wonder people who experience career boredom are more likely to fall into addictive and destructive behaviors. It can be a miserable existence when you find little to no positive feelings and experiences from your career, other than making money. You can have so much more from your job, and it is important to remember that career opportunities are closer than you think.

In an article written by Amy Joyce in *The Washington Post*, (August 10, 2005), she discussed boredom and how it relates to individuals who work on factory floors, in cubicles, all the way to the highest levels of any organization. She reports that senior officials in the U.S. government have actually run into each other while attempting to fit in an afternoon movie to seek relief from boredom. (The comments and sarcastic jokes I would love to make here are endless!) Career boredom applies equally to income level, marriage status, and living conditions. So whether you flew into work in your helicopter, slept in a 200-square-foot apartment last night, or you are Mr. or Ms. Middle Class, you are capable of experiencing the demoralizing phenomenon of career boredom and stagnation.

Are you bored yet? (Come on! That was hilarious!)

While it's important to understand what causes career boredom, it's more important to know what the steps are to overcome it. A client of mine provided a great example of overcoming career boredom. (I have changed his name to protect the innocent!) See if you don't recognize a little bit of yourself in Tim.

Tim had been laid off from a software firm several months earlier and was desperate to quickly find a new job. After numerous interviews, Tim accepted the first job offer he received and moved out West. Although he had interviewed with several firms, many of which he would rather have worked for, he took the first job offer solely based on his financial situation. Tim described his job as "Death by Boredom" after being there less than six months. Tim had tweaked his sleep schedule, realizing "the later I go to bed and the earlier I wake up means the more free time I have outside of work. I don't want to feel like my whole life consists of sleep and work." I decided to pry and find out if his work was really that bad.

Tim expressed that his career was going nowhere. He didn't see a way to increase his income or his responsibilities or get promoted. He felt stuck and the boredom was beginning to take a turn for the worse. He explained there were days in which he looked at the little clock on the corner of his computer monitor at least once every two minutes for the last hour of each day. 4:07 ... 4:09 ... 4:11, and so it went for the rest of the workday. Career Torture!

Tim recounted that recently all the staff in the office had been called into a meeting and told that new policies were going into effect. There was to be no cell phone usage during the day except for breaks. There was to be no Internet usage during the day for anything other than work-related activity. To put a cherry on top of the crazy sundae, Tim and the other employees were told there had been too much talking at work and the talking needed to stop unless it was work-related. Yes, a ban on talking. I was both amused and shocked! This office had a culture that would make a prisoner from the San Quentin state prison cringe.

"The worst part of all of this," Tim shared with me "is that I am already bored at work and these new policies are only going to make it worse. After we finish projects, we have a small period of down time before the next project rolls in. I go to the restroom five times a day just so I can check my personal email and texts to keep my sanity."

I shared with Tim that his description of work boredom was only a symptom of a larger problem. It had everything to do with a lack of meaning and purpose in his life. He agreed and freely admitted that the only reason he took this job was to make money and survive financially. I had to get Tim to stop thinking about his current situation and get him to focus on what actions he could take to change his circumstances. I introduced him to the Four Bash Career Boredom Tips.

Bash Boredom Tip #1

Take on a Challenge or Learn Something New.   When you experience career boredom at work the *very* first thing you need to do is enrich the working environment with new levels of complexity and challenge. According to Mihaly Csikszentmihalyi, one of my favorite researchers, the best way to combat boredom at work is to learn something new or begin a new challenge. If you are experiencing bouts of career boredom, you need to jump in and find a new challenge at work. Ask yourself if there is anything more you can accomplish or if there are employees who may need your help. Can you learn something new or take on a project that will develop your skills and competencies and push you into different areas?

The British Psychology Society [1] reports in an article on their website that boredom is " … not the result of having nothing to do. It is very hard to come up with a situation where a person's options are so limited that he or she literally can do nothing. Rather, boredom stems from a situation where none of the possible things that a person can realistically do appeals to them. Boredom is thought by some to be a distinct emotional state in which the level of stimulation is perceived as unsatisfactorily low."

---

[1] thepsychologist.bps.org.uk

To increase the level of brain and emotional stimulation and dispel career boredom, you need to find a challenge and learn something new at work. This approach works for about half of my clients, as some only needed a jump-start to get them moving out of the rut and continuing on with the great career they had already created. For the other half that don't find success, there's Tip #2.

Bash Boredom Tip #2

Find Meaning and Purpose Outside of the Work Environment. If you can't find challenge or meaning at work, your next step is to look for it outside of your work environment. There are numerous areas in your life that can fill the void of career boredom. Before you give up on your current position, it is well worth it to see if you can curb your career boredom with activities outside of work that provide the stimulation you are looking for. Tim was up for the challenge. He agreed to try a new focus outside of work.

Tim had earned a bachelor's and a master's degree in his early twenties. After his schooling, he specialized in one specific aspect of the software industry, which unknowingly at the time had limited the growth potential for his career. Tim knew if he decided to go to another organization it would only mean the same job with relatively the same pay. Because of his unique situation, he didn't see any benefit to changing careers. After understanding his situation, I agreed with him. After 15 years in the same industry, Tim knew his job well and there was little left to learn and improve upon. My goal was to get Tim to look outside the walls of his work to find something that could compensate for the deficits in his current career. I had a great idea to help him maneuver past the three problems with which he was grappling:

Problem number one: Tim was bored at work. Problem two: Tim didn't feel like he was progressing in his career. Problem three: Tim felt his career up to now had no real meaning and purpose. These three problems were wreaking havoc on Tim's professional life, but all three concerns could be solved by one big, giant action step. Tim had gone to law school after completing his master's degree but never took the bar exam. "How about studying for the bar and taking it in four months?" I asked him. The suggestion caught Tim by such surprise you would have thought I had just delivered him a right hook to the jaw. "I thought I would never go back and take the bar. It hasn't even been on my radar," Tim said. So I told him several reasons why it was such a fantastic idea.

Tim had gone to law school, spent $100,000 getting an education, and never taken the bar exam. That type of behavior is not good for the mind or the soul. He had left something he had heavily invested in half completed and it was holding him back. He needed to begin applying the knowledge he had learned whether or not he was going to practice law. Tim had to take the bar and we both knew it.

Taking the bar would require Tim to study. It would require effort and sacrifice. It would be challenging. He would have to stretch and grow. Another benefit would be the opportunities and choices that would come to Tim after he passed the bar (no matter whether he had to take it once or three times). After two weeks of thinking about it, Tim signed up for the bar exam.

The moment Tim started studying (think progression, purpose, and meaning!) I stopped hearing about how bored Tim was at work. He no longer complained about his job. (Every once in a while I would hear something … but everyone has to share the crazy things that happen at work, right?) Tim had a new sense of purpose and felt like he was progressing. Make no mistake that it was hard: hard for him to study after work, hard to give up his activities and his weekends. I told Tim I didn't care. Great things happen in a person's life when they put aside what they want now for who and what they want to be in the future. To put the whole experience in perspective, Tim was studying for only four months. It wasn't like he was being asked to learn Japanese and bind his feet from a size 14 to a size 7, although I did recommend it for the sake of his future wife. "Cry me a river," I told Tim more than once when he told me he was sick of studying. But notice he was no longer complaining about his job!

Tim went from career boredom and feeling stuck to progressing and having hope in the future of his career. I realize Tim's example is extreme, but the lesson is still important. If you, like Tim, are bored with your career, then new opportunities for growth may be exactly the remedy. Look for something outside of work that will provide your life with meaning, purpose, and fulfillment. Join a club, learn a sport, play the piano, grow a garden, volunteer your time, learn how to cook, or play cards with your friends. Numerous clients give so much time and hard work to their careers that they never realize that the small things that are missing could make all the difference. Making new friendships, having time to pursue a hobby, and creating something like art, food, or writing is often all that is needed to rejuvenate both your life and your job. Try it! You might be surprised by the effect it has on your work and life.

Bash Boredom Tip #3

You May Have Outgrown Your Job: Get Promoted or Move to Another Department. "It isn't me!" you say. "I would never want to be promoted or change departments. I love what I do!" Yet, you will sit right next to me and tell me how bored you are and how ready you are for a change and that you don't know how much longer you can do the same job. You would rather stay miserable in your current situation than make a switch to something different that you might actually like more.

Here are the signs you have outgrown your job and that it might be time for something else:

- You enjoy your job, but it doesn't provide nearly the satisfaction it used to.
- You find yourself getting antsy at work. You can no longer just do the same job every day. It is too easy.
- You find yourself checking the organization's job postings.
- You don't have an excitement for the role and the work like you once did.
- You are becoming territorial at work. You fight over the little things instead of looking at the big picture.

It is easy to implement the tips to combat this kind of boredom. It only requires some time and investigative work to decide what you want your next step to be. First, begin to gather information and look at jobs in your organization that would interest you. Match your skills sets and competencies against the job postings' requirements. Assess what you can bring to the positions and whether it would be a good fit with the culture, the team, and manager of that division or department.

Second, you need to begin networking and growing your brand in the organization so other leaders know who you are and will be more open to interviewing you for a position outside of your normal department. It is easy to tell yourself that your excellent work speaks for itself. It does, but only to a point. You need to build relationships with those who are the decision makers. Don't quite know how to do it? We'll discuss how to network in Chapter 16.

Third, learn as much as you can about the positions you are interested in. See if you can spend a few hours or half a day with the individual who currently works in that role to see if the role is exactly what you think it is and if you would be a good fit for the position.

Bash Boredom Tip #4

Time to Move on to Something New.   You have reached the end of your rope and you are burned out. You are ready to claw your eyes out rather than go to work. One of my clients described it best when she said, "I should be in the TV show *The Walking Dead*. That perfectly describes my work life. I go through the motions day after day after day. Even the salary no longer makes staying here worthwhile." If any of this sounds familiar, it may be time for you to move on, begin a new chapter, and find a new position. It can be difficult when you come to the final realization that you no longer just want a change, but actually ***need*** one. It is hard to close one chapter of your life and start another, but when done correctly and with the right preparation, it is easier than you think.

Assignment:

Write down any reasons you may be experiencing career boredom. Once you have identified the issues, look at each of the Bash Boredom Tips and decide which one to put into action.

Reasons I May Be Experiencing Career Boredom:

1.

2.

3.

4.

5.

Action Steps I Will Take in the Next Two Weeks to Bash Career Boredom

1.

2.

3.

4.

Recap:

1. Career boredom is different from normal boredom. It can cause various mental, emotional, and physical symptoms.

2. Your career boredom originates from a lack of personal purpose, meaning, and motivation toward your career. How to Bash Boredom Tips:

3. How to Bash boredom tips include:
   a. Take on a Challenge or Learn Something New.
   b. Find Meaning and Purpose Outside of the Work Environment.
   c. Get Promoted or Move to Another Department.
   d. Move on to Something New.

CHAPTER

7

Redefine *Rich*

Here is something to think about: How come you never see a headline like "Psychic Wins Lottery"?

—Jay Leno

Rich is a state of mind that should be nurtured before the money comes.

—Lonnie Rush

was flying to San Francisco for meetings when he sat down next to me. He exuded success and money. He couldn't have been a day over 30 and was dressed impeccably well—not in a tailored suit, but in a more casual style that said, "I don't have to wear a suit." He wore his new Apple Watch and was busy flipping through his messages on his phone when he leaned over and said to me, "I hate it when I can't get a hold of my virtual assistant."

"Local or international?" I jokingly asked, thinking I was funny.

"Both," he responded.

I knew I was supposed to be impressed so I introduced myself to Lincoln.

Lincoln was an Ivy League graduate who had done well in Silicon Valley when the start-up he worked for went public and he became an overnight multimillionaire. He was still working for the same company nearly a year and a half later but was thinking of starting the whole process over at a different start-up.

"Tell me the best part of your success story," I encouraged.

He described the months before the company went public, with all the work and excitement surrounding what this would mean financially to everyone at the organization.

"So now that you have got it made, what's the plan?"

By the look on his face, you would have thought I just sucker punched him. For a split second, Lincoln's demeanor changed and I saw a glimpse of indecision.

"I'm figuring that out right now," he said. "It's been a different ride than I expected. I'm having to circle back and figure out what I want to do."

I leaned in and said to Lincoln, "You're rich, just not the rich you thought you would be."

Defining *Rich*

What is rich? Society defines rich as a nice, large home, expensive cars, and extravagant vacations. Add on the country club memberships, grand pianos, and costly steak dinners while not forgetting the butlers, housekeepers, and personal drivers. For decades this has been the definition of rich. *Lifestyles of the Rich and Famous* with Robin Leach was a hit show in the 1980s and 1990s. I grew up spending an hour a week observing how the rich lived. That show inspired the poster that hung in my dorm room as a freshman in college. It was a picture of a mansion with five cars, all worth over $100, 000 parked in the garage. The caption read "Justification for Higher Education." *Rich* was about possessions: acquiring more and more, being the boss, and having authority.

"How will you know when you have made it?" I asked several friends. "What will you own, do, or experience that will make you feel like you are rich?"

"A boat" was one response.

"A Maserati" was another.

"A beach house on Coronado Island, California."

"Tour Europe for a month."

The answers came fast because they had already asked themselves that question many times before. The same goes for nearly every person I meet. Everyone has "something" they can identify that will make them feel like they are rich and have made it! Do you know what your answer would be?

But the meaning of the word *rich* is relative. Hopefully, after reading this chapter you will change your perception of what rich actually means to you. You may find you don't really want what you think you do. Instead of viewing rich in terms of money, power, and things, let's view rich in terms of what matters most to you. Let's dive into four areas that will help you figure out **your** own personal definition of rich. The key word in that sentence is **your**. Your rich is going to be different from everyone else's. This is something you definitely need to think about so you can quit chasing everyone else's definition and expectation of rich. This principle can be life-changing, so get ready for your brain to be infused with new ideas. I hope you walk away with a new paradigm about what constitutes your personal wealth and a greater understanding of what you really need from your career and life.

What Matters Most and What I Value

Before we can identify your definition of rich, we need to find out what you value and what motivates you to go to work each day. By being aware of your values and motivation, you can make choices that are in line with things that really matter to you. By knowing what matters most and what you value, you can strategically proceed through the three areas of being rich (feelings, money, and time).

I want you to brainstorm what things you value or what matters most in your life. Write them in any order and then number them, with "one" being the thing that matters the most to you. After you have numbered your list, I want you to write the why for each answer! Let me give you an example:

What Do I Value and What Matters the Most to Me? *Why*?

My family is a top priority to me.

Why? Because I love them. My relationships with them make me happy and bring fulfillment and joy to my life.

Now start your own list. Here are some examples of values to get you started. Feel free to add others to your list.

Family	Success	Creativity
Work	Spirituality	Volunteering
Money	Health	Security
Friends	Connections	Possessions
Free Time	Relationships	Love
Education/Learning	Service	Silence/Peace

What Do I Value and What Matters the Most to Me? *Why?*

1.

2.

3.

4.

5.

Knowing what matters the most to you will help you decide between competing priorities when it comes to your definition of rich. Let's move into the three areas of *rich!* (feelings, money, and time) so you can begin to understand **your** own version of rich.

Rich Is a Feeling, Not a Possession or Abundance of Stuff

I am a believer that most individuals really don't want to be millionaires. They want to *feel* like millionaires and have experiences that they mistakenly believe only millionaires can have. The desire is to live the life that being a multimillionaire would allow them to live: the freedom to travel or purchase without limits and the freedom from financial worries. Most of us view wealth as the ability to buy, to accumulate, and to have. We often buy things for reasons beyond the actual need of the item; we buy for the feeling it gives us. I know men and women who make millions and feel they have arrived. I also know individuals making the same amount who don't feel rich and are constantly seeking more wealth. I know people making $45,000 a year who feel they have hit the jackpot, while there are others making the same amount who are deeply unhappy and feel dirt poor. The secret is to understand what specifically makes you feel rich and to learn how to increase that feeling in your life.

When my wife and I bought our first home, I remember how rich I felt that first night. I couldn't have been happier in any bigger or better home. Looking back from a vantage point of 20 years, I recognize that it was a small home, but it provided us with a feeling of being rich. We felt like we had "made it." By becoming homeowners, we felt rich.

I asked one very wealthy individual what made him feel rich or when he knew he had made it. He responded, "When I get more." He knew he was wealthy, but he didn't ever feel rich. No matter how much he had, he always wanted more. Remember, rich is much more about a feeling than about your financial situation. Let me share an example:

It is time for a new family car. You have searched and found the perfect vehicle that fits your needs. It costs more money than you want to spend. Thinking of how you want to experience feeling rich, you look at your "What Do I Value and What Matters the Most to Me?" list. If you value time with your family and relationships, then why go spend an extra $20,000 for that nicer car? That means you'll have to work harder or longer and have added stress when the car payment is due, each and every month! If your feeling of being rich is to have more free time to spend with your family, then find a vehicle that has most of the same amenities but costs less. That way you can afford it, you'll have that important time with your family, and you won't have added financial stress. That is your *rich*! You choose what matters most and what you value—what gives you more of the feeling you want.

One more example:

You feel rich when you have free time in the evenings and on weekends. It allows you to exercise, spend time at the lake, play tennis with friends, and have a happier, more fulfilled (your version of rich) life. Your boss approaches you with an opportunity for promotion. It means a raise and a great title, complete with a corner office. It also means you will have to work more nights and weekends with clients. You would love the extra money and the corner office instead of a cubicle. Go to your "What Do I Value and What Matters the Most to Me?" list and see what it tells you about your idea of *rich*. Is the extra $15,000 a year going to make you feel richer, or would the free time you have on the weekend mean more to you? Getting the hang of it? It is all about priorities and choices.

Warning: A problem I often encounter with the wealthy is the misalignment of their "What Do I Value and What Matters the Most to Me?" list with how they actually spend their money and time. If a senior executive's number one item on his or her list is family and other relationships and they travel four out of five days a week, there will be misalignment. When the two aspects don't match up, this creates unhappiness and the *rich* feeling goes away regardless of how much money you have. Don't believe me? Look at many of the lottery winners or T.V. and movie stars.

Money (Enough Is Enough)

There are very few people I meet who don't want to make more money. When I met Matt, I was pleasantly surprised by his responses to my question: "How much money do you want to make in the next few years?"

"I will be rich when I have more family-and-me time. *Rich* to me would be making $80,000 so I can pay all my bills and be left with enough income that I can choose to go paddle boarding at 2:00 in the afternoon and not have to be in an office from 7:30 to 5:30 every day. Forget the expensive car and the vacation house—I don't want that type of *rich*. That isn't rich to me. Eighty thousand dollars a year with a flexible schedule is my idea of rich."

In our pursuit of a better life, we often think an increase in salary means an increase to our happiness—that they are directly related. Instead, I want you to take a minute and think about what minimum salary you could earn and be happy. When is enough money enough? Unfortunately, it is ingrained in us to always be thinking and wanting more. I want you to look at your "What Do I Value and What Matters the Most to Me?" list. Based on the top five items, choose a salary (as low as possible) that would allow you to live comfortably and create the rich, fulfilled life that you want. (This is going to cause your brain to freak out!) This is difficult for most people because we can't imagine giving up our current lifestyle. One of many lessons I have learned working with people who have recently lost their job is that they can survive off much less than they ever thought possible and that they are usually still happy. The exercise of determining your minimum salary will move you away from "more is better" thinking to a "what do I need to let go of to feel rich" mentality.

Let me share a personal example. When my two oldest daughters were preteens, they began an Olympic diving training program at one of the local colleges that not only had the springboards, but also the one-, three-, and five-meter platforms. International coaches were brought in to help the program grow, and the U.S. National Diving Association invested in dry ground equipment to train on. It was becoming a top-notch training facility.

My girls had a talent for the sport and excelled immediately. Diving coaches from universities around the United States would scout at their competitions I knew I was in hook, line, and sinker when three coaches spoke to me about my daughters and said if they continued on the path they were on, they would get full-ride scholarships to any school of their choice that had a diving program. (One of the coaches was from Harvard!) It was an exciting time, but with one problem. The facility was an hour from our home. This meant that the moment school let out until late in the evening, we were on the road or at practice. There was no time for other sports, homework, or piano lessons. After a year, we felt anything but rich. There was no happiness in the long drives and the stress of completing schoolwork after long workouts. While the girls loved the sport, the sacrifice was too steep. So we all decided that the girls would choose another sport. Within one week, we felt rich! It was like we won the lottery and had our lives back. Everyone was much happier. The lesson was learned that sometimes cutting back, while getting or doing less, actually increases **your** feeling of *rich*.

Oftentimes we think we need more money to feel rich. If our meaning of *rich* has very little to do with money and more to do with relationships or experiences, we may be surprised that a realignment of our schedules to match our priorities may give us greater feelings of wealth (rich) without actually changing our income.

If you earn $80,000 a year and you knew you could find another position in your company with less responsibility, fewer work hours, and have a more flexible schedule and make $60,000, would taking that job be worth it to you? It was to Matt—that is why everyone has a different *rich*. What is important to Matt may not be important and of value to you. An increase in wealth is not directly proportional to your feelings of wealth. When I started my own business, I took a major pay cut from my corporate job. The flexibility that self-employment gave me, however, allowed me to spend more time with my wife and kids, which I hadn't done in a long time. This made me feel infinitely richer and happier.

Time

Time is one of your most precious resources. Everyone I know has 24 hours a day to spend the way they choose. Those who feel rich choose wisely how and where they give their time. Be very careful when others ask for this precious resource. We often say, "yes" to things that we later regret. If someone walked up to you and asked you for $30, would you hand it over without a second thought? … No? Think of how carelessly you give away 30 minutes of your day.

An acquaintance of mine told me a story about how he chose his career. When he was a teenager, his father chose to go to law school later in life. This was a difficult road and required my friend's father to be gone frequently. After graduating from law school, the father started his own firm and had to work long hours to build his clientele. While this was a dream for his father, it was difficult for my friend. Later, when my friend became a father himself, he decided he wanted to be more involved in his own family's life. He chose a sales career in which he would have flexibility to attend his children's sporting events and activities. That was what he valued the most and what made him feel rich. No amount of money could substitute the joy of watching his kids play soccer. He found the "lasting rich" feeling is based on fulfillment of your values and not necessarily derived from money.

Redefining *Rich*

As the plane prepared to land, Lincoln and I found we had talked most of the flight. He admitted he now had a much different view of his career and future than he did at the beginning of the flight. I admitted I had a much different view of him—that I really didn't like him when he first sat down next to me. We had a good laugh, and as we departed, I wished him luck on his journey to *feeling* rich. (I later regretted not getting his card to send him a bill for two hours of free career counseling. He was monetarily *rich*, after all!)

All three factors, feelings, money, and time, play a role in how rich you really are. Think carefully about what you value and what aspects of your career you need to maintain or change. The best part of Redefining Your *Rich* is that you are in control and can choose the outcome that you want. If things aren't the way you want them, then decide to make a change.

As I thought back to that first house and how rich we felt, my wife and I discussed how we don't feel any happier or any richer than we did at that time. We may have moved up in the type of house we own but it hasn't changed our feeling of being rich.

Recap:

1. What do you value? By knowing what matters most, you can make choices in each of the three areas of your *rich* (money, time, feeling).

2. *Rich* is a feeling, not an abundance of stuff. The secret is to understand what makes you feel rich—what provides you that feeling and how to increase it in your life.

3. Decide now how much money you need to make you happy and fulfilled. Set a realistic goal so that you can open up opportunities in time, relationships, and career. More money doesn't necessarily mean more happiness or more *rich*.

4. Time is your greatest resource. Be very careful how you spend it. Truly rich people guard their time and how they spend it.

8

Why You Are NOT Stuck in Your Career: The Power of Change

My favorite fruit is grapes. Because with grapes, you always get another chance. If you have a crappy apple or peach, you're stuck with that crappy piece of fruit. But if you have a crappy grape, you just move on to the next one. Grapes: The Fruit of Hope.

—Demetri Martin

Do You Feel You Are Stuck?

Most of my clients can easily identify when they are stuck. The problem comes in figuring out *why* they feel stuck and *what* they can do about it.

The *Why* of Stuck: Quit Being Helpless

"But I am *stuck*, Dr. Bray," Lisa yelled at me. (Yes, she did yell!) "I can't leave my job because I have kids, a mortgage, bills, car payments, and responsibilities … " … Blah, blah, blah. Lisa then proceeded to list every reason she could remotely think of why she was stuck in her life. They were all good reasons why she couldn't change her current situation. "Help me get unstuck!" she pleaded.

So I went drastic with her. She needed to be reminded of her power to choose in order to change the paradigm of her career.

Me: Lisa, does anyone hold a gun to your head to make you go to work every day?

Lisa: No.

Me: If you quit tomorrow, would the business fold?

Lisa: No.

Me: Do you get chained to your desk once you get to work?

Lisa: No.

Me: So you actually choose to go to work every day?

Lisa: I don't choose. The bills, the mortgage, and the kids choose for me. (I loved her answer! It was the essence of her problem!)

Me: So there is no other job or department in your company? There is no other job in your city other than your current one? This is the only place in your company or the only place in your city that will pay you for your skills?

Lisa: Yes. There are other places to work and other departments I could possibly transfer to, but I would have to change jobs.

Me: Yes, you would have to change.

Lisa: I don't like change.

Me: So there it is! You hate change. You aren't stuck; you just don't want to change. Well, neither does most of the world. Yet, people manage to do it every day. It's time to get over your fear of change, take action and get unstuck. If your current situation is that miserable, it just might be worth the effort!

Embracing Change

In many of my seminars, I ask participants to raise their hands if they perform their current job the exact same way they did five years ago. Only about one or two out of every hundred people raise their hands. I then ask them to compare how they performed their job three years ago compared to today. Only about 30 percent say they do their job the same way they did three years ago. So, according to my rough poll, that means the job you do today is going to be significantly different in less than three years. This means you will need to continually learn, improve, and adjust your skills to meet the needs of a changing role. Change is a constant. The problem is most of us don't like change.

You're Not Stuck—You Can Change Positions within Your Company

Recently, I worked with an individual who has been in banking and finance for over 20 years. In that time, he has been in three completely different segments of the banking industry that had no direct relation to one another. He shared that he "never expected his career to be so full of change," but he now sees those changes have been a benefit to his career and income. He has become more experienced and valuable as an employee with each new set of responsibilities. So remember—you are *not* stuck, but you might need to do some changing.

You're Not Stuck in One Career Forever

My clients often tell me—"Change wouldn't be hard if I knew the next job or promotion was going to be better than what I have now." I always tell them—"Start the journey and you'll figure it out as you go. Make a choice, move ahead with confidence and the road will appear."

"I have taken three career assessments, three personality tests, and met with two career counselors," Andy told me. "According to all the interviews I've done, they tell me it is clear I would make a fantastic accountant. Nearly every assessment and test is pointing me toward this type of work. But to be realistic, Dr. Bray, I don't know if being an accountant really fits my personality. I like the numbers part and the process aspect, but the thought of sitting at a desk all day is not what I want to do for the rest of my career. I have worked as a volunteer firefighter in the past and that was a job I really enjoyed. I know accountants make more money than firemen, but I'm not sure what I should do. I'm stuck. Which direction do you think I should go?"

I didn't need to think before I responded to that question! If any career counselor within a 10-mile radius of me could have heard what I said, they would have rolled their eyes in disgust and shoved a career assessment right down my throat to gag and silence me from ever speaking such career heresy again. I told Andy, "You may be well suited to several different jobs. So you can take either job, you can take both jobs, or you can find some completely different job in a totally separate market segment. Why? Because, like most people, you are not going to have just one career for the rest of your life. Life doesn't work that way anymore. You will likely have numerous jobs and they are all going to have positive and negative aspects to them. As you progress through your career, you are going to identify what things you like about each job and what particular aspects you don't like. With each new job, you should be moving toward getting more of the positives and less of the negatives. That is called career development. It's part of the process of finding your Best Job Ever!

"If you want to be a fire fighter, go be a fire fighter. If after three or four years of running into burning houses, you decide you want to get an accountant job and sit in a safe building, then make a change at that point. Will there be consequences to that way of thinking? For sure, but they will not be as bad as you think. One of the Big Five accounting firms may not hire you, but I know lots of mid-sized companies that would hire a fire fighter accountant. As a fire fighter, you may initially make $15,000 less per year than you would as an accountant but that may be worth having had your stint as a fire fighter. I would take $15,000 less to have the chance to run into a burning building and save someone!"

To clarify, I'm not saying everyone needs to jump ship and leave his or her company. You may have just as many opportunities inside your current organization as you would outside of it. I worked for a Fortune 100 company for 12 years and had six different positions, some of which I sought and some of which came looking for me. The key for me was not to get stuck, but to expand my skills and increase what I could offer the organization. The same goes for you. As you progress throughout your career and increase your competencies, the time will come when the positives far outweigh the negatives and you'll find yourself happy and fulfilled with the work you are doing daily.

The Truth About Being Stuck

You are not stuck. You have the power to choose and to change.

I will say it 10,000 times: you are *not* stuck in one career field for the rest of your life. The knowledge and experience that you collect, the expertise and skills you master can be related to numerous different fields. The leadership skills you develop in sales will be just as effective for being a leader in the technology field. If you have been successful in customer service and now want to move into the marketing department of your company, it is possible. In fact, more and more organizations are assigning brief work stints in different parts of the organization to give future leaders a broader sense of the company. It is much more common in the last decade to see successful individuals move to different parts of an organization. The key is, you need to be a successful employee so that other doors will be opened for you. You also need to have done some networking within that department so they know you and you know them. Yes, it may be more difficult than taking the traditional route but transitioning to other departments will serve you well as your career progresses.

Look at your career more as a climbing wall than as a ladder. You may need to step down, move sideways, and then climb back up.

For example, a Fortune 50 company I recently worked with promoted a very successful salesperson into the product department. He brought valuable expertise and knowledge to a department that didn't have much interaction with the field force. By collaborating with the field force to gather feedback, he has helped that department make a significant difference in what they offer other parts of the organization. He brought together two departments that had previously worked in a silo mentality. It helped the company and helped his own branding and career.

Another example is Kate, who decided to return to the workforce after 20 years of staying home to raise her children. Not sure what she could offer a company and a bit timid about her skills, she took a lower-level position in the communications department. Within three years, she had been promoted twice. Everyone wanted to work with Kate on projects. Not only were the projects always successful, everyone also enjoyed working on her team. She laughed and told me, "This is nothing compared to the mayhem of having three kids under five years old for 24 hours a day. An angry executive is easy to handle in comparison. I learned valuable lessons at home that have served me well in corporate America." Companies have quickly come to understand that many of the skills that have made an individual successful in the past are transferable to other parts of their organization.

1. Do you feel stuck? Yes or No?
2. What are the top five reasons you feel stuck?
   a.
   b.
   c.
   d.
   e.

Now that you have identified the reasons you feel stuck, you are prepared for Part Three, which will empower you to make whatever changes are necessary to become unstuck.

Recap:

1. You are not stuck! There are always options and different directions you can take in your career.

2. You will likely have numerous jobs throughout your career. Embrace change and the opportunities to learn new skills sets and competencies.

3. Job skills you develop can be transferable to numerous areas of your organization.

CHAPTER
9

What Career and Life Do You Want and Why?

What lies behind us and what lies before us are tiny matters compared to what lies within us.

—Ralph Waldo Emerson

E veryone has those days—the days when you sit at your desk and ask yourself, "What am I doing with my life? Why do I come to work every day? I don't like it, I'm not appreciated, my voice is not heard and I do the same thing day after day." Pushing the "what am I doing?" thoughts out of your mind, you head to the vending machine for some chips or a sweet treat, telling yourself it is only a bad day; tomorrow will be better. You lie to yourself, saying, "I am going to do something about this. Tomorrow I will start figuring out what I want to do with my career and my life." You return to your cubicle munching on your chips, feeling better that tomorrow you are going to start figuring out your future. Yes, tomorrow will be the start of something really great in your life.

Then tomorrow turns into next week, and next week turns into next month, and the months turn into years as you consistently ignore those nagging feelings that something needs to change. You may feel disappointed you have waited so long to recognize that something wasn't quite right with your career. You may be sad because you think there's a possibility you have wasted years of your life. You may feel despondent as you think of what might have been had you taken a different course in life, so you cover the feelings by keeping yourself so busy you don't have time to feel anything. You convince yourself that things at work aren't that bad and at least you have a job. You tell yourself a long list of stories as to why you can't make a change and how it wouldn't work anyway.

If your work life is monotonous and dissatisfying, the time has come to decide whether to stay in your current life or to make some changes, switch it up, and create a career and life you love and are proud of.

Now is the time to find your purpose and meaning in the work you do every day. The life-altering question of "What should I do with my career and life?" will help shed light on your current situation. What used to be important may no longer be so. Suddenly, your happiness may mean more than your income. It may not matter if you are a leader or an individual contributor at work. What will matter is that you feel like you are making a difference no matter what your title. It doesn't matter if you have a nice car, nice house, or just the right clothes! What matters is that you are proud of who you are and what you have accomplished. You may now need things you didn't need in the past: meaning, purpose, fulfillment, and a sense of happiness at work. You need more than money, more than status, and more than recognition. This may be your wake-up call!

"What do you want from your career and life?"

"Where do you want to be in one year, in three years, and in five years with your career, life, and finances?"

These are two questions I have asked thousands of individuals over the past few years. Here are some of the most common answers I hear:

"Make more money."

"Get promoted."

"Don't get fired or laid off."

"Be more secure in my finances."

"Find a job I really like and enjoy."

Yet, none of the preceding comments is the response that I hear the most.

What is the most common answer to the question: What do you want from your career and life and where do you want to be in one year, in three years and in five years?

"I Don't Know!"

Hearing the answer of *"**I don't know**"* is difficult because I know the consequences of that statement in your life. You are so busy working, checking off your to-do list, picking up kids, doing the laundry, and keeping your boss happy that you have no time left to figure out what you want from your career and life.

Most of my clients are reluctant to admit they have no career strategy and instead choose to live each day, turning a blind eye to the future of their career. It is much easier to maintain the status quo and continue to do what you have done for the last few years, rather than take control and personal accountability to finally go after what you really want. This takes you back to the root of the problem: You don't know what you want, and if you do know, you probably don't know how you are going to get it!

Within minutes of my initial discussion with clients, they often tell me they want to leave their current organization for something new and give me all the reasons that back up that decision. Three or four months later, more than 85 percent of my clients decide to stay in their current organization because they find out what they *really want* is not far from what they already have—they just didn't see it or realize it.

I would bet 20 bucks you know what your ideal weight is, the next model of car you want, places you want to go on vacation, and when the next big game is on television. The unimportant things in your life are usually planned and crossed off your to-do list, while the critical life and career planning often gets neglected. Ask yourself this very important question: "Am I headed in the right direction for my career, for my family, for my personal life, and for my finances?

Don't cheat yourself by refusing to ask the really hard questions. I have worked with too many individuals who neglected their careers and paid the price in later years for refusing to take off the blinders that blocked them from seeing what was really going on.

"But I have time, Dr. Bray. I'm only 37 years old!"

Then in the blink of an eye, you get up one morning, five years have flown by like a speeding train, and you are 42 and in the exact same place you started. Much like it was for my friend Claire.

I met Claire during one of my career and leadership conference presentations. I began the presentation by asking the "Where do you want to be?" questions and the response from the crowd was dead silence. (It was 8:00 in the morning, so the silence was not unexpected.) Wanting to jump-start everyone's brains and get them engaged, I changed the topic to money! Everyone likes to talk about money. "How much money or what salary would you need to make in a year to be satisfied and happy?" "Would $40,000 be enough?" Silence ...

"Would $80,000 be enough?"

A few people raised their hands.

"What about $100,000 dollars a year? Would you be satisfied with that chunk of change?" At this question, nearly 75 percent of the group raised their hands. Now that we were talking about money, people began to get excited. Then Claire raised her hand from the back of the room and provided me with a light bulb "aha!" moment that drastically changed how I work with organizations and individuals. Claire was a bright, enthusiastic woman in her early forties (both her yellow suit jacket and her big smile exuded brightness). Claire said, "I don't know the exact salary number. I've never really thought about it seriously other than to always want more money than I currently make." She continued, "I have always wanted to try something new, like possibly getting promoted or changing departments. I always thought I could put it off until next year when I would have more time or after I had finished this or that project. I've realized recently I never did anything or made any changes because I *don't know how* to change. That is why I am here! I only wish I would have come five years sooner."

The room came alive and everyone started nodding their heads in agreement. They all knew they wanted to make more money, they all knew they wanted to develop their careers, *only they didn't know where to begin or **how** to do it.*

Since I had a willing participant, I asked Claire a follow-up question. "What do you want from your career in the next three years and what scares you about planning it?" Her response was classic. "First of all, I want to have a job." (Great answer!) "Second, I would like to make some changes and possibly get promoted, but I am not sure the money would be worth the added responsibility. I also don't know what else may be possible." More nodding of heads came from the group and others began speaking up, saying:

"I'm too busy with work and life to have time to make a plan."

"What else would I do for work?"

"I don't know how to develop my career. I'm in my forties and a bit too old for that."

"I don't know what options I have to make more money."

"I have put in so much time at this company. I could never leave now no matter how much I don't like it."

"It is scary to think of changing."

"What if I don't like my new job? I know that the grass isn't always greener on the other side."

"I don't even know where to begin. It is overwhelming to me."

"I just put my head down and go to work. I try not to think about whether or not I like it." (This was one of my favorite comments as I sometimes wish I had the ostrich-esque ability of long-term avoidance.)

These are all valid concerns and comments! The "*why*" behind what you want for your career can be more important than the "*what*." Planning and strategizing your life and career is not difficult. It only requires a little time and a computer or pen and paper. So grab either and let's get started.

Let's start this journey with the same steps I discussed with Claire and her group. I will take you through the five steps to build the foundation of your career development. In completing these five steps, we will determine your "career capital"—a great word I am borrowing from Cal Newport, one of my favorite university professors and career researchers. To get the most out of these steps and to find out what you really want from your career and life, you are going to need a little privacy and quiet time to come up with your answers.

You will find you don't have to write a lot—I want you instead to *think* a lot. Scary for some of us, I know, but wiping off those brain cobwebs and spending time thinking about this often-neglected topic is CRUCIAL to your future career and life success. It is imperative that you don't skip over this step, as it is the foundation to creating the career and life that you want. I will give you the questions and all you need to do is answer honestly. This can be difficult, as Mark Twain explained when he said, "We do not deal much in facts when we are contemplating ourselves." Each step will build upon the next and by the time you finish this chapter, you are going to have a real good feel for which direction you need to head with your career. This is a step-by-step approach that builds upon itself, so make sure you don't skip and jump around. Answer the questions as you read the chapter. (Meaning make sure you answer them right now!) Buckle up! This is the beginning of change for the better.

Step One: Your Current Career

If we are going to plan out your career and where you want it to be in the future, the first thing you need to do is take a good, hard look at where you are currently. You need to know the good, the bad, and the ugly of the career you have created.

When you start taking a good look at your career, I hope you find positive career experiences; a great network of friends and associates; challenging, fun, and purposeful work; fair compensation; and progression with your skills and competencies.

These are the things great careers are made of. Now if you are shaking your head and feeling like I am talking about the Land of Oz compared to your career, don't feel like you are alone in this. Nearly 85 percent of workers feel the same as you do! They are disengaged and dislike their jobs, so you have more company than you think.

One of the most difficult aspects of looking at your current life and career is that you get a glimpse of choices you have made that created a career or life you may not like or may not be proud of. It's discouraging to realize we may have taken a road or made choices that were not the best for us. You may have had a terrible event happen in your life that knocked you flat to the ground and it has taken some time to get back up.

Whatever the reason, you need to see a clear picture of your current situation so you can see what needs to be changed or improved. I want you to answer the questions below as honestly as you can. Write down quick bullet point answers. (Those are the best.) Don't overthink the answers or write a novel. Jot down answers as quickly as you can after reading the question. Ready to begin? Let's get started.

Step One Questions.

1. On a scale of one to five, how satisfied are you with your current job? (Five being if you won the lottery, you would stay working and one being you have to medicate yourself before you walk into the office.) Why do you feel that way?

2. On a scale of one to five, do you enjoy the culture of the organization? Is it a positive environment and are there opportunities for growth and development?

3. Do you generally enjoy the people you work with or do you find yourself wanting to key their cars as you leave? (On a scale of 1-5)

4. Do you feel your salary matches your role? (Now I get that everyone is going to say, "no" because you feel you deserve more, but in general, looking at individuals in your field, are you paid in line with similar jobs?) This question is about fair pay, not more pay. If you want more pay, keep reading and we will discuss ways to increase your income.

Notice that I am covering all aspects of your job. The work you do every day, the people you work with, your financial situation, the work environment, and opportunities for development. This should give you some good insight into where you currently stand in relation to your job.

Step Two: Define Your Career

Defining your Best Ever career is a tricky proposition and it is important to understand why before you continue. I have found the exercise of choosing a career to be one of the most difficult assignments I ask my clients or those who attend my workshops to complete. This is because defining what you want for the future (which is an unknown) has some innate problems. First, it is hard to choose something you may not know everything about (promotion, new job, new boss, and so forth).

Second, you know everything you *don't* want in a career, but you haven't figured out what you *do* want. You know you don't want a psychotic, micromanaging boss, ... you know you don't want to work 80 hours a week ... and you are sure you don't want to sit next to Sheila, who talks nonstop. But you have no idea what job you would like in five years. Give it some thought. This is where you need to get specific. Do you want to go from making $9 an hour to $15, or own two stores instead of one? Do you want to run your department or division or are you happy in your current individual contributor position?

You have to be the one to figure out what YOU want, but I WILL help you get there since the process is similar for everyone!

Think of the last time you pulled out your earphones and they were tangled so badly you thought that it was going to be impossible to ever untangle them. What is the first thing that everyone does with a knotted mess? We shake it! We think if we violently shake the earphones, they will untangle. It never works, and more often than *knot* (yes, I just did that and if you didn't get the joke, go ask your three-year-old neighbor and he or she will explain it to you), it binds the knot even tighter. As soon as we realize this, something in our brain enlightens us and we carefully begin working the knot and detailing the path that we need to take to get it untied. We trace each section to see where it goes and where it needs to be and which parts of the cord that we need to tug, nudge, or push through a small opening in order to disentangle the dilemma. As we continue attempting to fix the earphones we end up with smaller knots or more minuscule issues, and gradually, as we work through those issues, the string becomes more and more its untangled self.

I always wonder how a string or cord sits dormant and becomes knotted in the first place. How sitting in my gym bag or backpack, the earphones get that horribly tangled. Your career is like the tangled earphones. As you sit dormant, you become more invested in your current rut and get more and more tangled, unable to see how to get untangled and straighten things out.

To become untangled, you are going to need small steps, nudges, and pulls in the right direction, and maybe even some violent shaking here and there to get you to your goal. So my desire through this chapter is to get you to assess the size of the knot you have created in your career.

Suppose that you are a shuttle driver making $10 an hour and you love everything about the company and your co-workers but you simply want to make more money. Your career evaluation definition will have to include questions such as: Do I want to always be a shuttle driver, but just make more money? Do I want a new position that will offer me more money but stay with the same company? Do I want to own the company? (Yes, I want you to think realistically but I also want you to understand that in this book I want you to think big.) Let's say the shuttle driver answered the question by stating that he wants to own the company. Good for him! There are going to be some questions that need to be answered to define his goals and ambitions of owning the company. He is going to have to work, act, and plan differently than if he were to decide he loves his job and only wants to increase his salary from $9 an hour to $12 an hour. Each goal would require different behaviors.

Step Two is divided into three separate questions sets: A, B, and C. To fully answer Step Two, we need to delve into several topics.

Step Two Question Set A. Let's start off with pie-in-the-sky thinking.

1. If you could **be** *anything*, what would you be?

2. If you could **do** *anything*, what would you do?

3. Do you remember who you wanted to be like when you grew up and what you wanted to do with your life? Do you remember what things you wanted to accomplish? With your wise and experienced teenage brain (dripping sarcasm), what were your plans and dreams for your career?

4. If you knew you could not fail, what would you attempt with your career and life? Would it be in the same field as you currently work in or would it be something completely different from what you do now? Would it be starting your own business?

Write down in bullet point form as much information about your dream career that you possibly can. Let me share some good starting-point questions about your dream career to get your brain running.

5. Describe your dream Best Job Ever:

   - Do you work in an office or at home?
   - Do you work with the public or only individuals in the organization?
   - Do you work in a cubicle by yourself or are you working as a member of a team or a mixture of both?
   - Do you own your own business or work for someone else?
   - How much money are you making?
   - Is there a specific industry you are working in?
   - Are you a manager or an individual contributor?
   - Are you working for a small company, a large Fortune 500 organization, or for yourself?
   - What is the best part about your work?
   - Do you have people working for you?

The more information you can write down to describe your perfect career, the easier the other steps will be. Did you ever read those Choose Your Own Adventure books as a child? You are literally living inside one as you complete these exercises.

Dream Job

Step Two Question Set B.   Now that you are on a roll, write down the perfect job in your current market segment or organization. If you work in sales, write down what you would consider the best job in sales. If you think of a current position in your organization or in a different company, great. If your dream job doesn't currently exist in your organization, then bullet-point between 5 and 10 aspects of a perfect position. Answer the same questions from Step Two Question Set A #5 "Describe your dream Best Job Ever" but this time you are talking about your dream job in the company you now work for or in your current market segment.

Let's return back to the story of Claire and the career workshop.

The discussion amongst the group was becoming lively. A young man, no older than 30, asked a question that I could tell was important by his very serious face and concerned tone. His question was one of the catalysts for me to begin creating the Career and Life Revolution:

"Dr. Bray, you work with lots of people. Do you know of anyone who really loves his or her job? Is it possible to have a job that you love and enjoy, while still making a good living and not working your life away?"

I am a firm believer in the idea of "no dumb questions" but I will admit this one bothered me—not that it was dumb but because it made me reflect back on certain times in my life when I had the same questions. Like the young man, most of the workshop attendees believed this was asking for something impossible from their careers.

The young man was dressed in what I am sure was his nicest suit, and I could tell he was honestly eager to learn how to climb the corporate ladder and progress in his career. His question had no malice, but it left me wondering how many of us really believe we can find a job that we like, that produces a good income, that has a larger purpose that includes working with people we enjoy. This young man had been in the working world for less than a decade and already had resigned himself to work at a job he didn't really like, maybe even hated, just so he could earn a dollar.

So he could ...

- Have insurance.
- Tell people he worked at that really cool office downtown that gave him free lunch each day. (Yes, I do hear that quite often.)
- Afford to drive the nice car.
- Feel like he was keeping up with his friends by getting a job that paid more than $35,000 a year right out of college.
- Tell his parents he "managed people" and was a leader.

We all have reasons why we work—many of which are valid. But oftentimes, as I have learned from clients, we work for very different reasons. As most of us would agree, we work to pay for food, clothing, shelter, transportation, and other bills. But we also work for numerous other reasons of which we may not even be aware. We work certain jobs because that may be the expectation of others—mom and dad love that you are a pharmacist because it was always their dream! Or we choose a certain career because of the self-worth we gain from our job and job title. Or we choose a job based on the social network of friends we can make at work.

I have six kids and you better believe I need insurance when they get sick or crash on their bikes and break an arm. That is a necessity at my house and I have to find a way to always have insurance. But I have learned to not make career decisions based on one benefit or perk. I can find a job with insurance in many places while there would be few jobs that would provide career fulfillment for me. I can find ways to make money, but career happiness is much more difficult to come by.

"But *none* of those things matter if you have bills to pay!"

One of my clients said this to me ... and he wasn't the only one who has made that declaration over the years. It is a commonly repeated statement about careers and I would consider it one of the most valid. How do you balance the desire to have a dream career with all of the financial responsibilities you have in life? The argument of chasing your dreams versus being responsible is a reasonable point. But deep inside—don't you think it is possible to create a career that is able to do both: pay the bills and give meaning and fulfillment? **That is what this book is all about!** By answering the questions in this and other chapters, you will begin to create a plan that will map out your path to your Best Job Ever.

So if you want to run a scuba shop on the beach in Costa Rica or you want to be a vice president in corporate America, you need to have a clear vision and plan for your career. This plan will need to include a financial strategy, an understanding of your skill sets and competencies (what you are good at doing), and a dash of passion (meaning purpose and fun) to complete your career soup of success.

Step Two Question Set C. What education, training, and experience are you going to need to make your answers from Step One Questions and Step Two Questions actually happen?

What is the time frame you want this to occur in? Unless returning to school is on the list, I suggest the maximum time frame be two to three years. Accurately predicting much further out than three years with all the changes in organizations, technology, knowledge, and leadership is not realistic.

Are you willing to do what it takes to make your ideal career happen? Are you willing to put in the time, the work, and the effort? Take a full 24 hours to think about whether or not this journey is worth it for you. It is a difficult journey and can be rough at times. However, it is possible to create a career you love that is both financially and emotionally rewarding. Thousands of individuals have done it before you, including me. (This sounds like we are at the start of a *Lord of the Rings* movie!)

You have done it! You have completed the foundation of career development and taken the first few steps of developing your career. Don't worry if it doesn't feel concrete or complete at this time—that will happen as you progress through the next few chapters.

Recap:

1. **Step One: Your Current Career**. If you are going to plan out your career and where you want it to be in the future, the first thing you need to do is take a good hard look at where you are currently. You need to know the good, the bad, and the ugly of the career you have already created.

2. **Step Two: Define Your Career.** You need to know what you want in a career and what you don't. If you could have any job, what would that job be? What would you consider to be your perfect job in your current organization? You must decide what your ideal career looks like so you will be able to find or create it.

10

You Can Follow Your Passion Without Quitting Your Job

Be careful of following your passion. Dorothy followed hers and she ended up being so poor she had to kill a woman to get her shoes.

—Unknown

D ave was a dentist for more than 25 years when he decided to sell his practice and move to a small town in Alberta, Canada, to open greenhouses so he could grow and sell organic fruits and vegetables.

Shawn left an accounting career—where he was on track to make partner—so he could become a real estate agent.

Julie left her finance career so she could make jewelry and sell it on the Internet.

All three of these individuals had reasons they wanted to leave their jobs and chase after their dreams. The most common reason why they could no longer stay in their previous job was their deep desire to "follow their passion." They had to "make a go of their dreams." Each of these individuals introduced at the beginning of this chapter experienced what it was like to leave their jobs and *follow their passion*! They described their experiences in actually *following their passion* as: "exciting, nerve wracking, an immense amount of work, and more disappointment than they had ever before experienced." They also said the experience was "more fulfilling than anything they had ever before accomplished." Some individuals were successful, while others experienced failure. Some of them wished they had never left their corporate jobs, while others told me they would "never go back to working for someone else."

The Enticement of Follow-Your-Passion Jobs

Business magazines, websites, blogs, and TED talks often portray the image that "following your passion" in your career is the only way to go for happiness, wealth, and eternal bliss. In a moving commencement speech at Stanford University in 2005, Steve Jobs told the graduates to "Follow your passion and don't settle for anything less." The students and faculty were so moved they gave him a standing ovation. Soon after, the video of his speech was posted on YouTube and a decade later the video had over 19 million views. What was the crux of his message that resonated so well with the Stanford graduates?

"You can do what you love and be successful."

What a motivating, inspiring, and rousing message. How can anyone not get excited when hearing stories and examples of others who have followed their passion, made a difference, and become financially successful? We all want to believe that the world is our oyster and all we have to do is find what we love to do, start doing it, and we will make money, be happy, and enjoy the success.

More individuals than ever are taking the leap out of corporate America to chase their career passion. But before you jump in with the crowd too quickly to follow this Pied Piper, you need more information.

If you have worked for someone else, you are keenly aware that certain aspects of the working world can be difficult. Sometimes these challenges can create a belief that you can't follow your passion unless you quit your job and do your own thing. That is *false*! We may have this belief because the "follow your passion" theory is presented as an either/or proposition.

Either follow your passion and work for yourself *or* work for someone else and give up on all your dreams.

You need to know that in a majority of cases, you can follow your passion while keeping the job you have right now. That way you can have what matters most to you without all the sacrifices and risks of quitting your current job.

Having a passion for your work is important! Figuring out what you love about your job, what excites you, and what you want is vitally important to your happiness. The more you match your passion to your career, the better off you are going to be. If the follow-your-passion theory holds true, you will more likely be successful in your work. *But* the follow-your-passion theory for careers has some downsides you need to watch out for.

Obstacles to Following Your Passion

It makes complete sense that the more passionate you are about something and the more you invest in it, the more successful you will be. Except that isn't always the case. There are some obstacles with a passion-based business of which you need to be aware.

Let me explain:

The "follow-your-passion" theory is based on four steps:

1. Identify what in life you are passionate about.
2. Try to match your passion with a career that most coincides with your identified passions. (If you can't find a good job match, start your own business.)
3. Have the courage to quit your job and follow your passion.
4. Make money at your passion.

It sounds so easy, doesn't it? This kind of work life appears so fun, exciting, and fulfilling that the idea of working in a cubicle sounds like a prison. However, the follow-your-passion plan often doesn't work out, leaving the person unable to pay for house payments or rent, car loans, and all the family bills.

A woman working in corporate America has always wanted to write a book so she quits her job to have time to write.

A man loves building and fixing things around the house and is highly skilled at it. He decides to open up a handyman business.

Then … the book gets written and only a few copies are sold or the handyman doesn't get enough customers. The bills don't get paid and within a few months both are back at their corporate jobs feeling like they failed. They ask themselves: What went wrong? They followed their passion, but couldn't make enough money. Just because you are an expert in a certain area, or it comes easy to you, and you are passionate about it, doesn't mean you can make a living from it. Oftentimes those passions are called *hobbies* instead of careers! I am passionate about tennis, but I won't be on the pro tour anytime soon. Anyone in his or her right mind would not pay me a cent to give them tennis lessons.

Another obstacle is not knowing what your passions may be in the first place. If you have not identified your passions, discovering them may take time. You may be unsure of what you are passionate about. So sit back, put your feet up (unless you are on a plane), and let me share the steps to discovering and following your passion without quitting your job.

Find the Right Passion

It is absolutely possible for *everyone* to discover and follow their passion if done the right way! Identifying and implementing your passion in your career is a process that takes some time, but can have fantastic results. Finding a career that matches what you love is a process. Be prepared to invest the necessary time and effort into finding what your passion is and then have the courage to blend it with your current life and work. When we speak about a passion, it doesn't necessarily mean making a handicraft or playing a sport. It may mean that you feel passionately about spending as much time with your family as possible. For you, the job of a teacher may be fulfilling that passion because of a shorter workday that allows you to be home earlier. Perhaps your passion is acquiring knowledge, or traveling, or volunteering for a cause.

The Three Steps to Following Your Passion without Quitting Your Day Job

Step One: Identify the Aspects You Love about Your Current Position

It is important to discover what you are passionate about in your current job. You should be able to easily identify what you enjoy about your job, what comes easy to you, and what you have mastered, all by just being aware of your daily routine. Observe yourself for a week and take notice of what tasks, projects, or jobs you excel at. Which tasks or activities do you finish much faster than others? What responsibilities at work cause time to fly? Another clue may be areas of your work where you are considered an expert and other employees come to you for help and assistance.

Passion often comes from mastery. People are passionate about what they are good at. (Except for golf, which is an exception to this rule.) Ask children if they enjoy practicing the piano, and they will tell you they hate it. But once they master a difficult piece, perform it, and receive a round of applause, all of a sudden they enjoy practicing and playing the piano. It is called *mastery-induced passion*. Over the years, numerous individuals who previously felt they needed a change in their job, decided to stay and focus on mastering their current job. In so doing, they felt a renewed sense of fulfillment and satisfaction in a job they had previously disliked.

If you have been unable to determine what you love about your job, what you feel passionate about in your work, or what you excel in, then give yourself a full week of observation time. If, after a week of observing, all you come up with is your passion for your lunch hour, then you need to ask a co-worker who knows you well or someone you trust, to give you some feedback that is honest and forthright. Let me share an example to get your brain in the mode to recognize your talents and what you are passionate about.

My first job out of college was working for a pharmaceutical company. I am to this day deeply grateful to Woody (yes, he is from the South!) who gave me the opportunity to work for a Fortune 100 company. This job meant I could start paying off my student loans and supporting my family. Corporate America was new and exciting and I loved every part of it.

After a few years passed and I had been promoted, I began noticing aspects of the job that I didn't enjoy: tasks that I dreaded to work on and only completed because I knew I would get in trouble if I didn't finish them on time. I hated the paperwork, the weekly reports, and expense sheets. I would rather pull my teeth out than look over all the numbers on the reports. Also, the conference calls were painful and seemed to last much longer than was needed.

On the flip side, I began to notice what I loved about my job. I loved the people I worked with and my customer visits and interactions. I enjoyed the teaching aspect of my job and relished the opportunity to help new reps learn, thus decreasing the time it took them to become successful. I enjoyed working outside and not being confined to an office. Most importantly, I discovered that I had a strong interest in the behavioral side of corporate America: figuring out what motivated my team, learning how to get them to perform at a higher level, and teaching them to deal successfully with internal conflict. I learned through experience what came naturally to me and what I was really good at. This self-awareness led me to the idea of returning back to school so I could study these topics.

I learned:

- I didn't want to work in an office.
- I enjoyed interacting with customers and other employees.
- I loved organizational development. (Even though I didn't have any idea what it was called at the time.)
- I had a strong interest in finding out what motivates people and why they react how they do in certain work situations.
- I learned that teaching, helping, and training were some of my strengths.

Step Two: Identify the Parts of Your Job You Dislike and Acknowledge the Gaps

This step is going to hurt a bit. I know—I have done it myself and assisted lots of others in going through this particular process. This next step is to get really honest with yourself and document what is missing from your job—the things you really value but don't have—the *gaps*.

Also, you'll need to determine what is plain terrible about your current role and *why*? (See end of Chapter 2—you've already started a list of reasons you are disengaged from your job. You can expand upon the list with this step.)

Ask yourself: *What don't I like about my job? Do I like the people I work with? Do I like my boss?* Don't give me your dislike of the week, look beyond what is currently bothering you, and decipher the long-term negatives about your job. Write down each concern under that answer and then give the reason *why* you dislike it or why this is a gap for you. For example:

What You Don't Like: I don't like that I have a weekly call with my boss reporting what I have completed during the week. I have been at the organization for five years and I am competent at my job.

Why? It makes me feel that I am not trusted and I don't know my job. It also makes me feel like my boss thinks I am incompetent.

What You Don't Like: I don't like that I have to play politics at work to get ahead. That kind of behavior drives me crazy.

Why? It makes me feel like the only way to get promoted is to kiss up and be one of the boss's favorites. It makes me feel like my hard work and success don't mean anything unless I play the game.

What You Don't Like: I prefer working with others but my job requires me to work alone or be in a cubicle most of the day.

Why? I value collaborating with others. I work best discussing and bouncing ideas off others. I like interacting with others and experiencing a team success.

Don't let emotions interfere with this part of the process. You may feel overwhelmed by focusing on the negative, but it is only for a small fraction of time. The information you gather will provide invaluable insight! The purpose of this exercise is to help you figure out what is really important: what you love and what may be missing.

Step Three: Determine What Is Negotiable and What Is Not Negotiable

Step Three requires you to decide what aspects of your current role are negotiable and which ones are non-negotiable. First, take your list from Step One—The Aspects You Love about Your Current Position— and circle those items that are non-negotiable for you. These are aspects of your job you must have to be happy and feel fulfilled. For example, one of my non-negotiables is that I choose not to work in an office all day. Since my first job out of college, I have never worked in an office. I know I am not happy and at my best when I have to be in an office environment every day. (I also get more done. I'm the guy who likes to chat with everyone in the office.) I could have made significantly more money if I had taken an office job, but the extra money was not worth it to me. It was a non-negotiable.

Now put a checkmark to the side of the items that are negotiable for you in a career. What aspects of your job are you willing to possibly bend for if given the right incentive? I have a colleague who despises traveling for work but when he was offered a job as a director, he decided that his desire to not travel was negotiable based on the benefits of the job he was being offered. He decided he could travel for two years to obtain the title and experience he would need to progress in his career. Travel was a negotiable for my colleague at this time in his career based upon his needs and wants.

What Needs to Change?

Once you have your list of negotiables and non-negotiables, put a star next to the items that you feel you or your boss can change. What is within your or your boss's circle of influence to change? Don't make assumptions! You might be surprised by your power and influence to initiate change. Once again, this is about gathering information and not about making a decision. I am asking you to notice the aspects of your career and job that are missing and might require some attention.

Often, when a client reviews this part of the gap list he or she tells me, "Dr. Bray, I have to change jobs. This job doesn't give me three weeks of vacation and I have to have three weeks of vacation." You may be surprised what you can get changed at your work by asking for it. (Especially if you are a high-performing employee.) Maybe instead of a raise this year, you can ask for an extra week of vacation. How about asking for extra projects to earn that extra week of work? Unfortunately, most minds don't think this way. I can already hear you saying, *"This is not going to work."* I have lots of examples of when clients said the same thing and I proved them wrong. Ask and negotiate and you will be surprised at how often you can work out a deal, especially if you are a top performer! If you are not a top performer, spend four to six months becoming one before you ask for any changes to your current work situation. I can promise you no company is going to go the extra mile for you if you haven't gone the extra mile for them.

Conclusion

Don't think because you don't like your current job you are failing in your career journey. You need to use your current position as a stepping-stone to finding out what you are passionate about.

I know it's more romantic to picture yourself singing *"Take this job and shove it"* as you walk out the door to start your Fro Yo Shop. (I love frozen yogurt and I have always wanted to open a shop at the strip mall down the street so I'd have never-ending access to yogurt as well as a built-in job for my kids.)

But …

Don't throw your job away until you have discovered where your passion lies and figured out if it can be found or created within your current job.

Step 1: Identify the Aspects of Your Career That You Love

1.

2.

3.

4.

5.

Step 2: Identify the Parts of Your Job You Dislike and the Gaps

1. Why?

2. Why?

3. Why?

4. Why?

5. Why?

Step 3: Decide What Is Negotiable and What Is Not Negotiable

1. Circle the Non-Negotiables.
2. Put a checkmark next to your Negotiables.
3. Put a star next to items you or your boss have the power to change.

11

Career Plan Step #1: What Is Your Job?

I love asking kids what they want to be when they grow up because I'm still looking for ideas.

—Unknown

When I was a pharmaceutical salesman in my twenties, one of the accounts assigned to me was the Oklahoma prison system. I remember being extremely excited (that is an understatement) to call on the prison doctor and get my first experience behind bars.

As I walked to the doctor's office, I couldn't help but notice the inmates were in handcuffs and foot shackles with chains. Every time they moved the rustling of the chains was a reminder of where I was. For days, I couldn't get the image out of my mind and wondered what life would be like to wear handcuffs and foot shackles everywhere I went.

I have since learned that most of us have our own set of handcuffs and foot shackles. (Oftentimes, we put them on ourselves and don't need a warden.) When we leave the house in the morning, we make sure we have our chains on to slow us down throughout the day, strip away our joy, and hinder the pursuit of our goals. These shackles of fear, excuses, and not knowing how to move forward serve as constant reminders of past bad experiences, failures, and of not ever "being enough."

How you deal with these chains will be a determining factor in the success of your personal and professional life. The purpose of this book is to help you identify what those chains may be (Part One: Why You May Feel Stuck in Your Career), teaching you how to break free (Part Two: Why Your Best Job Ever! Is within Your Reach), and now showing you how to begin to create the career and life you want (Part Three: Planning to Create Your Career).

In the previous chapters, you have learned tools to identify and overcome career fears and excuses while identifying what specifically you want from your career and life. We have talked about what may be holding you back from achieving your greatest career goals and desires and the power you have to change yourself and your circumstances. You now have the knowledge to make better decisions as you move forward.

As a young manager taking interviewing training, we were told that the "best predictor of future behavior is past behavior." That does not have to be your story or your experience. I choose to live by Maya Angelou's quote, "I did then what I knew how to do. Now that I know better, I do better." You now know better, so you can choose better. This is Day One of a new chapter and a new history as you continue to change and work toward your goals. It will not be easy, but you can do hard things.

Anything worth doing is hard. That is what gives you the feeling of accomplishment and progress. In our family, we have a motto that states: "Brays can do hard things." Anytime a difficult situation presents itself, one of us is going to say, "We can do hard things." And guess what, we do! And if we fail? We say we tried, we learned, and the next time we will be able to do better. Life is about becoming better, not being perfect and successful every time. Some friends and acquaintances have told me this type of thinking is positive self-affirmation and doesn't work. I disagree. I think it is the best way to learn how to deal with life.

What Is Your Job?

The first step in creating your career development plan is determining the four most important responsibilities of your current job. What is the bulk of work you focus on every day? To be clear, I'm not asking for tasks you complete. I want to know, the main responsibilities of your job. For example, if you are a manager, one of your main responsibilities is leading your team. The tasks associated with that responsibility would include communicating with your team, providing resources, and setting deadlines for projects. Tasks are much different from responsibilities. When I ask this question, most of the responses I receive are more task-related than role-related. A second response I often get is, "I don't know exactly what I do every day, but I am sooooooo, sooooooo busy!"

If your answers are similar to these examples, you need to take a step back for a few days and observe what you actually do on a daily basis. Some of you may laugh and say, "Who doesn't know what they do every day?" But what you say you do and what you actually spend your time doing may be completely different.

An HR recruiter I consulted with provides an excellent example. She had always liked her job but was becoming increasingly unhappy with it. We started off by discussing her one-, three-, and five-year plan (we'll do this in Chapter 14) and then moved on to asking about her four main responsibilities at work. "I recruit top talent for the organization," she said. But when we discussed her position, her work, and daily activities, it quickly became apparent that her daily job didn't match her initial answer of recruiting top talent. When I shared my observation with her, she was not ready to hear it. "Of course my job is recruiting!" she said a bit loudly.

I decided to give her some time to reflect and encouraged her to observe her daily activities, write them down, and then we would discuss them the following week. When she returned, she hadn't even sat down in the chair when she emphatically stated, "Dr. Bray, I am not a recruiter! My title may say I am a recruiter but that is not what I do most of my day. We are short-staffed and I am spending most of my day taking care of HR issues and answering managers' HR questions. This leaves me no time for recruiting." (It is at moments like this that I *always* want to say, "I told you so," but that would be unprofessional.)

Career Development Plan

Step One: Key Roles at Work

What are the four main responsibilities of your job?

1.
2.
3.
4.

It's time to put all you've learned to good use and move into the implementation and action phase. Let's begin to build that career and life plan with Step One. Pull out the heavy-duty bolt cutter, free yourself from your chains, and let's get to work creating a career plan that will bring you closer to your Best Job Ever!

CHAPTER

12

Career Plan Step #2: Discover Your Strengths

Talent without discipline is like an octopus on roller skates. There's plenty of movement, but you never know if it is going to be forward, backwards, or sideways.

—H. Jackson Brown Jr.

I t was 2003 and social media was in its infancy. Tech companies were popping up by the dozens. One particular company was launching a new platform they hoped would prove to be a game changer. The organization had a plan to revolutionize music and podcasting. With an ex-Google leader on board, and numerous programming whiz kids, the company hoped to become one of Silicon Valley's next rising stars. By July 2005, the company, called Odeo, had a viable product and strong investors and was ready to launch. Then disaster struck in unprecedented proportions. An announcement from Apple changed the future of Odeo. Apple was launching a breakthrough product called iTunes to revolutionize the way people listened to and downloaded music. Along with the music, iTunes would also include a podcasting platform automatically built in to every one of the 200 million iPods Apple would sell. In one day, with one announcement, Odeo was considered finished.

With 14 full-time employees, the CEO and leadership team decided to exit the podcasting business and head in a different direction; they just didn't know which direction. In fact, they had no "Plan B" and time was short to develop a new product or platform.

To solve the problem, the company started holding "hackathons." Hackathons were full-day events in which employees would work only on new potential projects. As the projects began to develop and show promise, the individuals involved in the idea would form teams to continue development. One idea for a service revolved around individuals sharing with friends what they were doing at any given moment. It was a platform that allowed people to update friends on their current status. In February of 2006, the idea was far enough along that they decided to present it to everyone at the company.

Originally, the idea was a system in which you could send a text to one number and it would be broadcasted to your friends, but evolved into a social site where you could follow friends' short updates and they could follow yours. It was initially known as Twttr, but the name would later be changed to Twitter. At this time of writing, the company is worth *5 billion dollars* and is only expected to continue to grow.

Case studies from top business schools have analyzed and explained Twitter and the process of their reinvention, but I see the event differently than most. When Apple announced iTunes,

Odeo knew it was over; they were out of business. Instead of focusing on improving or modifying their current platform (and in some way try to salvage all the work they had done), they did something I consider brilliant. They pulled their employees together—employees who were smart, creative and talented—and told them they needed to help create a new business model. Few companies do that today. Instead, most leaders close the business and start over when everything goes south.

It was an exciting time at Twitter. Employees were paid to use their strengths and talents to create something new. Twitter is an example that great things can happen in your career and life when you tap into your inner strengths and talents. The cherry on top is that in so doing you will also create career happiness, fulfillment, and a sense of purpose.

What Are Your Strengths?

"Dr. Bray, I have no idea what my strengths are, let alone how I can put them to use."

According to Gallup,[1] strengths are defined as, "the ability to consistently provide near-perfect performance in a specific activity." I would add that strengths are something that comes easy to you, you are naturally good at, and you find interest and enjoyment in. Strengths include your talents, skills, knowledge, and (some) personality traits.

Several thoughts are hopefully popping into your mind about what your strengths may be. A few clients have come up with their own original strengths:

"I am good at napping." (I think that is considered a universal strength! And it doesn't make you stand out.)

---

[1] "Strengths Dashboard," What Is a Strength? Accessed October 4, 2015. http://strengths.gallup.com/help/general/125540/strength.aspx.

"I am really good at video games." (I didn't consider video games strength for this 36-year-old father of three—and neither did his wife. Although the amount of hours he spent practicing were commendable! And yes, kudos to me for saving a marriage!)

"My strength is the ability to almost read people's minds with my intuition." (After laughing out loud at what I thought was a really funny joke, I realized she was dead serious. I badly wanted to ask her why she needed my help if she already knew what I was thinking, but I missed the opportunity and have regretted it ever since.)

Another client responded with, "I am really talented at cleaning my car. I even Q-Tip the vents." I once again laughed out loud, after which he told me he was somewhat offended. I told him the answer was so good I wanted his permission to put it into my book. He agreed.

Identifying your strengths and talents will help you recognize what specific traits and abilities you possess that help you stand out from everyone else.

Identifying Your Strengths and Talents

Recognizing your strengths can sometimes be difficult to do on your own. To solve the problem, here are three suggestions to easily pinpoint your strengths.

Option One, take the StrengthFinders 2.0 assessment by Tom Rath. StrengthFinders 2.0 provides an assessment that is excellent at finding what your five core strengths are in the work environment. It provides you with insight and in-depth information that helps you focus on your strong points. (Warning: If you are buying the StrengthFinders 2.0 book used, be sure that you find out if the assessment number has already been used. Each book has one assessment number that can be used only once.)

Option Two, ask your boss, your fellow employees, good friends, and even your loved ones what strengths they notice about you. What makes you stand out at work and what are you really good at? Be sure to ask people whom you trust to provide you with straightforward and sincere feedback.

Option Three, take a personality test (as I recommended in Chapter 5). I highly recommend the DiSC profile or MBTI. Both of these personality assessments help to increase your self-awareness, identify your motivations, and recognize how you react to problems and how you solve them.

Combine this with the strengths assessment and you will have a strong indication of what type of personality you have and how well it matches your current position. From the MBTI, you will learn whether you are an extrovert, introvert, thinker, or feeler (along with other traits). From the DiSC profile, you will learn about your behavioral differences in the following four areas: dominance, influence, steadiness, and conscientiousness.

This information will provide you with a glimpse into your behaviors and the manner in which you work. People who use their strengths and talents at work have been shown to be happier about their job, work environment, and co-workers.

Building Strengths and Talents

A debate has been raging the past 10 years or so over whether employees should focus on developing their strengths or working to improve their weaknesses. The correct answer is both.

It is important to build your strengths, while also monitoring areas that may keep your career from progressing. When you do work that is consistently using your strengths and abilities, you will be fulfilled and happy, and continue to progress. It is also important to work on your weaknesses and find ways to minimize their effects on your career. We all have aspects of the job we detest; sometimes that's the nature of the job. Other times we detest parts of our work because they play into our weaknesses. If we aren't aware of our weaknesses, they can become career killers. You may have incredible talents and abilities at work, but if you can't get your reports in on time, your other strengths are negated. Your objective is to be constantly developing your strengths and abilities while continually minimizing your weaknesses.

Jackie, a top salesperson in her company, lost $25,000 of her bonus because she received a B rating on her end-of-year review, instead of an A rating. She was shocked to receive the lower evaluation, as her sales had remained in the top 10 percent of her company. When she questioned the lower rating, her manager explained that she had submitted only three reports on time the whole year. Even though her sales were phenomenal, she was unable to complete her work in a timely manner. "You are lucky I gave you a B and not a lower rating," he told Jackie.

Even though she was the top salesperson on her team, Jackie was no longer considered a top performer. Her inability to complete and turn reports in on time had affected her branding, her year-end rating, and ultimately her bonus. An old-school human resources and training department would say, "Teach her how to do it correctly, help her plan and schedule time to complete her reports during the day, and strategically help her understand how to focus on the right tasks." However, that would put the responsibility back on her managers when the responsibility should rest squarely on Jackie's shoulders. I would tell Jackie that she will never, not ever, *like* completing expense reports, but they are an important part of her job that she must follow through on. Did she need to become the best employee at filling out expense reports and help other members of the team with theirs? *No way!* She needed to find a way to minimize her problem and it was an easy answer. "Get your reports in on time and make sure they are done correctly.... It is that simple," I told Jackie. "By doing this simple monthly activity, it will solve your bonus problem, your B rating problem, and get you back in good graces with your manager."

It's Time to Compare

Once you have identified your strengths, it is time to compare your four main job responsibilities (Chapter 11) to the strengths you have identified in this chapter. Does the work you do every day match your identified strengths or are there inconsistencies between the two? Comparing the two just might surprise you, but it may also give you the information you need to make changes (if needed) or to confirm you are on the right track with your career.

If you find that your strengths and your work responsibilities are polar opposites, keep reading for ideas of how to begin to align them in Chapter 14 when we discuss your one- three-, and five-year career plans.

Recap:

1. Identify your strengths. Take strengths assessment or talk to your fellow employees, boss, or family members to identify your talents, abilities, and personality strengths.

2. Take a personality assessment. Find out more about what makes you tick so you can identify the best type of work for your personality.

3. Compare your four main work responsibilities from Chapter 11 with the information you learned about your personality and your strengths. Is the job you are currently doing a good fit?

4. Remember the secret is to maximize your strengths while minimizing your weaknesses.

Resources

A link for a free resource to determine your strengths is freestrengthstest.workuno.com. It will take about 20 to 25 minutes to complete the assessment.

You can get a discount on the DiSC assessment by going to my website DrCkBray.com and going to the resource page for the link.

You can get a discount on the MBTI assessment by going to my website DrCkBray.com and going to the resource page for the link.

You can get a discount on the StrengthFinders 2.0 book by Tom Rath by going to my website DrCkBray.com and going to the resource page for the link.

CHAPTER

13

Career Plan Step #3: What Makes You Awesome at Work?

Excellence: "the quality of being outstanding or extremely good."
—Oxford Dictionary

I was bored out of my mind. I decided to do a late night gym session and discovered after five minutes I really didn't want to do anything. I didn't feel like getting on the hamster wheel (treadmill) or lifting weights (it was too late at night and my energy was all but gone) so I decided to hop on a new machine that I had no idea how to work, but had a redeeming quality I liked—a television screen! I figured the best way to get some exercise and distract myself for 30 minutes was to turn on a show.

I flipped through the channels and landed on the Time Life channel that was showing reruns of *The Carol Burnett Show* while also trying to sell me a DVD set for a mere $49.99. Within 10 seconds, I was hooked and ready to buy, but luckily I didn't have my wallet with me.

I was annoyingly laughing out loud (I couldn't help it) as Carol Burnett, Harvey Korman, and Tim Conway reenacted an office scene with a boss and his secretary. Some 30 years later, it was still great comedy. The legendary cast were masters at their craft. They made comedy look natural and easy and kept me laughing so hard I could barely stand up. As I watched, I was jealous that they were having such a good time. While driving home, I realized I loved *The Carol Burnett Show* because she was so good at what she did. Her excellence affected the lives of millions who had the opportunity to witness her brilliance.

I like seeing people excel after working hard to become their best. It is increasingly rare for people to invest their time and energy into becoming great at what they do. As I have watched and studied individuals who stand out in the workforce, I noticed that it doesn't matter the pay, the hours, or the work situation, these people always bring their A-game. (Even when they don't feel like it.) Developing awesomeness is the foundation for Step Three of the career development plan. We have identified your key roles and responsibilities, we know your strengths, now we need to find out the value you bring to your boss, your counterparts, your team, and the organization. When you leave work at the end of the day, what did you do that made you stand out among everyone else? In what areas do you excel in your current job?

Why Be Excellent at Work? Why Stand Out?

Mediocrity has become a bad word. It's not enough to be just average. As quotas increase and workloads spike, organizations have a compelling need for increased competencies and skill sets from employees. Those who are mediocre are getting left behind. But on the flip side, it is also becoming more difficult to stand out in the workplace as the expectation of job excellence and performance increase.

You already know the reasons you should be excellent at work. Standing out has its perks, such as the increased possibility for raises and promotional opportunities as the company increasingly values you and your work. While these are important, they are also shallow when compared to the long-term benefits excellence brings to your life and career.

When you are excellent in your work, you are building skills that will help you not only now, but also in the future. You are investing in yourself, and joy and fulfillment come from the process of working to become great.

What Value Do I Bring to My Company?

If you are confused as to what you excel in, or what value you bring to your job, this may be an initial bad sign! (Uh-oh!) Begin by considering your personal strengths and talents you identified in Chapter 12. If you still don't know what value you bring, quickly run and get your last performance review and search out what was written about you. What specific behaviors were documented that speak to where you excel in your position?

If nothing is in the performance review, you have your work cut out for you.

Grab your trusted fellow employees or others who work in your department and conduct several interviews with only one question: *What are one or two areas in my work that I am seen as the expert?* Listen closely and hope for the truth! If you don't agree with what they are saying, then you are probably correct in assuming they are not speaking the truth. (It is difficult to find people who will tell you the honest truth about yourself.)

Another method for discovering what value you provide is to listen to your fellow employees or customers when you return from vacation. While you were gone, what fell apart? What didn't get accomplished and what does no one else in the department know how to do as well as you?

Now that you are prepared, let's answer the question. Grab a pen or a pencil and write down what value you offer your direct manager, counterparts, and your team members! Write down at least three responses.

What Value Do I Bring to My Company?

1.

2.

3.

How Do I Become Excellent?

This is where it begins to get fun. If you can't identify an area in which you are already excellent, then choose one aspect of your work to become the expert in. Be sure that it is something you enjoy because you will be spending time on mastering this skill. Here are a few suggestions to speed up the mastering process.

1. Learn as much as you can about the area you want to excel in. Become the knowledge expert in that area.

2. Do more than is required for that specific responsibility. Go beyond being able to do it faster and better than anyone else. Think of what could go wrong or problems that are regularly seen in this area and be the one to provide suggestions on how to fix the issues.

3. Be the first to help others when it comes to this specific task. The more you practice, the faster you will master it.

4. Take the lead in this area. If any new project arises that pertains to this area, stand up and take a leadership role. If you are not chosen to lead, then be an active contributor and bring ideas to the table, and speak up when a bad idea is presented. You need to position yourself as an expert. Once you figure out how to excel in one area, it is much easier to do in another, not to mention that developing excellence becomes habit forming!

I Refuse to Broadcast My Successes

The time has long since passed (unfortunately) that your work speaks for itself. If your boss and others in your department and organization don't know how great you are, and what areas you excel in, you may be making a fatal career mistake. You have to stand out to be noticed, to get opportunities, and to increase your job security. (Not to mention earn more money!)

"But I hate to brag."

"I don't know how to market myself."

"I don't like yelling about my accomplishments from the rooftops. It makes me look like a kiss-up."

Most people find it difficult to tout their accomplishments. It is important to know that there is a big difference between bragging and creating a branding for yourself in the organization. You won't need to tell everyone about your recent success if others do it for you. By involving others in your work, you can congratulate and give kudos to them. It will make their day and they will do the same for you, giving you the recognition you've earned.

To be clear, the one person you must speak with about your accomplishments and successes is with your manager. It is your responsibility to set aside time during your one-on-ones to share what you are doing well. Your boss is not a mind reader, but is busy instead working and worrying about his or her own career. You need to provide the information so it can be shared up the leadership chain.

You have now completed the foundation of your career plan and it is time to start planning, strategizing, and creating the career that you want. This is where the fun begins!

CHAPTER

14

Career Plan Step #4: One-, Three-, and Five-Year Plan

Life isn't about finding yourself. Life is about creating yourself.
—George Bernard Shaw

One of the best parts of a vacation is planning it. Thinking about everything you want to do and places you want to see and all the fun you will have. This is exactly what we will do in creating your career plan. We are going to plan your career over the next year, three years, and five years. This is your chance to think, ponder, and decide what you want to do for the next few years. Remember, this is when the sky is the limit for you. During my workshops, everyone gets excited at this point in the day. We have looked at their past, diagnosed their present job, and it is

133

now time to plan for the future. When I tell the workshop attendees they have one hour to plan, the pens go in the hands, but they don't really start moving. After about five minutes, I begin to get comments and questions asking for help. "Dr. Bray, I'm not sure I know exactly what I want."

It's very likely you will face the same problem. It is easy for you to decide what you don't like. You may not like horror movies or vegetables. You know you don't want to work on skyscrapers washing windows. The difficulty comes in determining what you actually *do* want. This is where most individuals talk in generic terms. "I want to make more money" is one of the top answers on the board. (Yeah, I get it. We all do!) Some say they want to be promoted or manage people. All are vague answers with no specific information about the final destination they are trying to reach. The devil is in the details for Step Four and you may have to push yourself to answer the career planning questions. The more detail you include in your answers, the better off you are going to be.

"But Dr. Bray, nothing ever turns out like it is planned. Won't I be wasting my time doing this?"

Absolutely not! Without a plan in place you are nothing more than a paper boat heading down a river that will take you where it wants. If you have a plan that includes accurate information, you can steer your boat in the direction you want to go. Because life sometimes surprises us, you may need to adjust or adapt your plans for the future, but at least you'll know where you are headed. With a career plan in hand, you will be able to recognize opportunities as a means of getting closer to your goal or moving yourself away from it. Without that plan, career decisions may seem murky. Ben's situation is a perfect example.

Ben enjoyed his job but was becoming restless to take the next step with his career. We discussed the future of his career and what he envisioned. He bought into most of my suggestions but did not put the time, necessary effort, and thinking into his career development plan. Six months later, he called to tell me he was getting promoted. "Tell me, why are you taking the promotion, Ben?" I asked.

He responded, "It makes more money, I get to be a manager and I get out of here." Trying not to be a total Debbie Downer on his celebratory promotion announcement, I asked him one question: "Is the job helping you get closer to your five-year career plan?"

"It doesn't matter," he told me. "I can worry about that with my next promotion." I left it at that and didn't say anything more. I opened up my calendar and marked a date six months in the future and wrote his name on it. That is how long I gave him before I knew he would call me asking for help.

To my shock he lasted a full year before I received the phone call. Not surprisingly, Ben didn't like his job and needed help figuring out his next move. I politely told him to grab the career development plan, fill out Steps Four through Nine and call me when he was ready to take charge of his career. (He stayed angry for about two months before he called me back. I should have charged him double.)

Begin Planning

To get the most out of Step Four, I recommend you go somewhere quiet and peaceful. Try to get away from any distractions and turn off your phone. You need a chance to think about what you want your future to look like. Make sure you are in the right frame of mind and have a good attitude when answering the questions and planning your career. If you don't finish, don't let more than five days go by without working on your career plan, otherwise you'll lose momentum. Try to finish Step Four in one week. Remember, this is not meant to be a stressful experience, it should be enjoyable. So grab your favorite drink or snack and let's get to work.

I am going to ask you five questions about your career and what it will look like in one year, in three years, and in five years. Answer each question for each specific period.

Question #1

Will you be working for a company or working for yourself? Or are you doing both? Circle one of the options that follows for each period.

(Remember to answer this question for one year, for three years, and for five years.)

One Year	Three Years	Five Years
Company Self-Employed Both	Company Self-Employed Both	Company Self-Employed Both

This is important to know because it provides the framework for the direction you are going to take with your planning. If you know you want to work in corporate America in the next five years, then we will be able to move to the next step and identify what that job in corporate America would be. If you know you want to own your own business in five years, you are going to have to start taking some steps in that direction.

Many ask about the possibility of doing both. I know many individuals who like to do additional work on the weekends or during their evening time. Coaching community college soccer or creating a product to sell at the local farmers' market can all be done while still keeping your full-time job. For those who want to be entrepreneurs but don't want to risk leaving corporate America, this may be a great way to put your toe in the self-employment pond. Be sure that you are not breaking any contracts with your day job before deciding to do this!

If you are in a relationship, I highly recommend that you discuss this with that individual after completing all of the chapter questions. You will want his or her insight, opinion, and approval, or the outcome may not be a desirable one.

Question #2

What will be your role based on Question One?
Will you be promoted?
Will you stay in the same job?
Will you stay in the same company with a different job?
Will you have changed companies?

One Year	Three Years	Five Years
Role	Role	Role

The more detailed information you can provide, the better. This question always brings up unexpected emotions and thoughts.

"I can't see myself in that promoted position. I don't think it will ever happen."

"My boss isn't going anywhere. Her position will never be open."

Don't get caught up speculating whether or not something will happen. This part of the exercise is to help you determine

and plan what you *want* to occur. So leave all the doubts aside
and write down what you want to have happen.

Question #3

Do you manage people or are you an individual contributor?
Why?

One Year	Three Years	Five Years
In Management	In Management	In Management
Don't Manage	Don't Manage	Don't Manage

It is vital to identify whether or not you want to manage
people. Your salary, the location where you live, and other opportunities and perks are based on your answer. Managing is not for
everyone. There are lots of advantages to staying in an individual
contributor role. Don't grade the success of your career based on
whether or not you are a manager. You can be a leader within
your organization at any level. Remember, your true success is
based on how you define *rich*, which we discussed in Chapter 7.

Question #4

How much money will you be making?

One Year	Three Years	Five Years
$	$	$

This is an exciting topic because everyone likes to dream big
about how much money they can make. However, if you are currently making $22,000 a year, you need to be realistic about your

salary three years from now. I don't want to discourage you, so if you put down that you will be making $100,000 in Year Three, I am hoping you have a detailed plan in place for Question Five. If you're making $22,000 and want to more than quadruple your salary, you need to get promoted, go back to school, or find a position that has that kind of earning power. I have no qualms about putting a big number down in Year Three and Year Five, just have a strong plan to back it up. And if your plan is to marry rich or take out your spouse for the insurance money (or both!) move ahead as if neither are going to occur.

If you don't know how much money certain jobs make, you can go to Google and search out salary ranges for most positions. A specific company may pay more or less for the position, but this will give you an idea of the salary range.

Question #5

What are the talents, skills, and strengths or training and education you need to possess to make your career plan happen?

One Year	Three Years	Five Years
Skills	Skills	Skills
Training	Training	Training
Education	Education	Education
Other	Other	Other

Now is the time to decide how you are going to make your responses to the first four questions become a reality. This step requires some research into finding out as much information as possible about your future job. Talk to as many individuals as you can who may have information about the job you want. Not only will you learn what skills and competencies you need, you will also learn about the day-to-day responsibilities.

I also recommend looking at job boards and searching out jobs that have been posted for that position. Look for the training or education required in order to apply for the job. Then you can easily identify what skills sets you need to acquire or strengthen to make you a strong candidate for the position.

The question "What do I need to do to get the job?" causes some people to get a bit depressed when they realize the amount of work that is needed to progress toward that goal. This is a good time to decide whether or not it is worthwhile to pursue the job at this time. Think about it and discuss your hesitations (as well as what excites you) with your family and friends. Make sure you let the information simmer in your head for at least a few days before making a decision. Hearing yourself talk out the pros and cons will help you make the best decision.

A favorite client of mine is an incredible strategic thinker, leader, motivator, and coach. She is constantly sought out by her peers and also other leaders for her advice. She would make a fantastic senior leader but with two preteen children at home, she has made the decision that her definition of *rich* is having the opportunity to be home with them in the evening rather than traveling extensively as a leadership position would require. When looking at her one-year plan and three-year plan, her goals remain exactly the same as her present situation. It is her five-year plan that drastically changes. At that point, her children will be nearing graduation and a promotion and increased job responsibility will be more feasible for her and her family. The best part about this client is that she is consistently continuing to develop herself for the time when she can make the change. She has a list of what she needs to do and who she needs to become to be a stellar leader for that future position.

You may notice that I put "Other" in the worksheet as well. As you plan out your career, there may be something specific that you need to do to successfully get that position. That is the place to write it down so it is a constant reminder of the direction you are going.

Of all the questions, Question Five will take you the longest to complete. Don't give up! Keep reading and researching every-thing you can about your future job. Spend the necessary time and don't cheat yourself out of the opportunity to build the career that you want. The success or failure of your career depends heavily on the time you spend on this question and the informa-tion you are able to gather. As a helpful hint, don't spend more than two weeks on this question or you will begin to stall in your progression. There comes a point at which the amount of new information you are gathering drops dramatically.

Putting It All Together

Now let's wrap this up. You have identified in the future whether or not you will be working for an organization or for yourself. You have decided what the role will look like and what your specific position will be. You know whether you want to be a manager or not and you have decided on a compensation that fits your budget and the lifestyle you want. Lastly, you did your research and discovered what you need to do to get to your goal. Congrats for completing this chapter and making decisions on what you want your future to be.

15

Career Plan Step #5: The Big "Why?"

What you do matters, but why you do it matters so much more.

—Unknown

Finding why *is a process of discovery, not invention.*

—Simon Sinek

A century ago, the Wright brothers were in a fast and furious battle against numerous competitors to develop the first manned flying machine. One of their most prominent competitors was Samuel Pierpont Langley. Despite all of Langley's previous accomplishments, he felt he had not reached the pinnacle of his career. He wanted to be the first man to fly to help ensure his place in science history. He wanted to be considered in the same league as prominent earlier inventors like Alexander Graham Bell and Thomas Edison.

Langley seemed a sure winner in the race for flight. He had the notoriety, the financial backing, and all the right connections. The war department of the U.S. government provided $50,000 of funding for Langley to build his flying machine that he called an *aerodrome*. Because of the financial backing he received, he was able to hire the best minds. All of these advantages were topped off by the publicity his flying activities attracted. The *New York Times* followed him around and reported on every flying attempt he made. It seemed everyone was rooting for Langley to be the first to fly.

On October 7, 1903, Langley was ready to test his aerodrome. Mounted to the top of a houseboat on the Potomac River, the aerodrome was launched by a catapult and immediately crashed into the river. A reporter covering the flight said it flew, "like a handful of mortar."[1]

A second attempt was made two months later, but this also ended in failure when the aerodrome shot straight up in the air then dove right back into the water.

Meanwhile, in Dayton, Ohio, Orville and Wilbur Wright were underdogs in the race to fly. They seemed to be on the opposite side of the spectrum from Langley. They had very little money and financed the project on a shoestring budget they earned from their bicycle company. The *New York Times* provided no media coverage of their activities and not one of their team members had a college education. They were considered a pretty ragtag group. The only advantage they held over Langley was their passionate reason of *why* they wanted to fly. The Wright brothers simply loved the idea of flight and had no other motives

---

[1] Lianne Hansen, "The Race for Flight," NPR, October 19, 2003, www.npr .org/templates/story/story.php?storyId=1469463.

to fly. It was said that the Wright brothers took five sets of spare parts to each launch because they crashed so often, but they refused to quit trying. Nine days after Langley's second failed flight attempt, the Wright brothers took flight on December 17, 1903, in the hills of North Carolina. The brothers made four successful flights that day, thereby ensuring their names would go down in history.

The very day the Wright brothers took flight, Langley received word of their success and quit. He didn't attempt to improve upon the Wright brothers' design or learn from their knowledge and experience. Instead, he completely walked away from his goal. His *why* wasn't the joy of flying.

Despite everything being against Wilbur and Orville Wright, the one thing they had in their favor was a strong *why*, which was their deep desire to fly. It was their passion. They spent every possible moment thinking, talking, and inventing flight. They crashed, rebuilt, and flew again. They had no expectations of riches or fame as their reward was simply the opportunity to fly.

Understanding the *why* behind your career goals ensures you are on the right track for the long term. When you understand the *why*, you have a much deeper realization of the reasons you need to continue pushing forward or maybe the reasons you need to stop and head in a different direction.[2]

Knowing the *whys* will give you the strength to continue on when you might otherwise want to quit. A study was conducted of overweight men who decided to diet to lose weight. The men who wanted to lose weight so they could look better (get those six pack abs) were not as successful on their diets as those who decided to eat a healthier diet and exercise for family and health

---

[2] S. Sinek, S. *Start with Why: How Great Leaders Inspire Everyone to Take Action* (New York: Portfolio, 2009).

reasons. The men who focused on being healthy so they could coach their kids' soccer team or be more active with their loved ones had a much better rate of success

Few people have a clear understanding of why they do what they do. Our behaviors are often driven by expectations or habits, both of which become so routine that most of the time we are not even aware of why we are doing certain things. It will take some self-reflection to become aware of the motivations behind your behaviors and actions. Many of the people I have worked with thought they knew exactly what they wanted and why. But when I had them do a self-inventory of their goals, they had a few surprises.

Now it's your turn. Don't hold back on your answers. Each of the questions that follow will help you see your *why*; the real reasons behind what you do and what motivates you to continue on.

Write the first thing that comes to your mind.

1. How have you defined success in the past?
2. When you failed at something important, what did you tell yourself was the cause?
3. How will you know when you have made it? List three things, that when acquired or accomplished or experienced, will be a sign that you know you have reached the success you seek (for example, when you can afford to travel the world, or when you are able to give a certain amount to charity).
4. What is your main motivation for reaching your goals? Look at your strengths for a hint. Look beyond the reward of the goal and discover the personal reasons.
5. What will you get out of implementing your career plan? What will it do for you?

Knowing the motives behind your dreams and goals will help you overcome obstacles to your success.

Break It Down

Take each of the answers that you have written in Chapter 14 for your one-, three-, and five-year goals. Now, write down the *why* behind each of them. Take the necessary time to think about the truthfulness of each statement that you write. Make sure your motivations (the *whys*) are congruent with the long-term goals you have set.

One-Year Goals   The Whys for those Goals

Three-Year Goals   Why

Five-Year Goals   Why

CHAPTER

16

Career Plan Step #6: Your Community

True friends will always push you toward the great possibilities of your future.
False friends will always chain you to the mistakes in your past.

—Seth Brown

When we think about building our careers, we tend to focus solely on ourselves. We worry about having the right skills to match the job we want or exhibiting the right behaviors to prove we are ready to take on more responsibility. While we do everything we can to increase our chances of landing the right job or getting the promotion, we often forget what may be the best advantage we have: our community and network of friends and associates.

A past neighbor of mine, who I will call Alan, disappeared one day. Alan was what I call the neighborhood guy. He was the guy who knows everyone. Alan had a perfect lawn that he mowed twice a week. (There was no way he was trusting that job to anyone else!) There wasn't a golf course in the state that looked as good as Alan's lawn. He was always outside and I never passed his house when he wasn't there to give me a wave and a hello. Then one day Alan mysteriously disappeared.

I didn't notice for several days that Alan was missing until I saw that his lawn was looking overgrown and several dandelion weeds were popping up. I almost hit my brakes and screeched to a halt because dandelion weeds in Alan's yard must mean the world was coming to an end. I realized I hadn't seen Alan all that week. Something must be wrong.

So I stopped and knocked on Alan's door. When his wife answered, I jokingly said, "Something must be wrong because your lawn hasn't been mowed in days and you have dandelion weeds! I came to see why Alan is slacking."

She looked around (the kind of head turn that spies do when they are about to share secrets) and quietly said, "Alan lost his job last week. He has taken it really hard and doesn't want anyone to know. He is embarrassed," his wife shared. "He doesn't feel like seeing or talking to anyone right now."

As I drove home, I realized the most popular guy in the neighborhood, the guy who knows everyone and had a community of hundreds of people ready and willing to help him (if they had known his predicament) was instead choosing to isolate himself so he could take care of his situation alone. Noble in theory, but not wise in execution. When I returned to Alan's house the following day, he confided in me that he had lost his job and was worried. I made a few small suggestions to Alan to help with his career search. I encouraged him to be outside as much as he was in the past. I suggested every time someone stopped to talk to share his predicament and ask if they knew of contacts or opportunities. I also encouraged him to start calling and emailing all of his friends and contacts to ask for help in finding job opportunities. Alan decided to put aside his feelings of embarrassment and went to work networking. In less than a month and a half, he had a new job.

I can't stress enough the importance of spending the appropriate time and energy making sure you have the right connections and network. As you just read, Alan needed his community to help him. When it comes to developing and furthering your career, you, too, need your community to help you.

Networking Is Good … Networking Is Good (Repeat Three Times for Full Brainwash)

Networking. Most people hate this word and dislike the process of networking even more. "It feels shallow and manipulative, not to mention inauthentic and completely exhausting," I hear from clients on a regular basis. The thought of approaching someone you don't know at a business event and talking about the weather, sports, or the latest movie seems less enjoyable than poking your eyes out with an appetizer fork. You understand it is important to get to know more people and expand your circle of influence, but actually doing it can seem uncomfortable and self-serving.

But if done in the right way, networking is about building relationships in an authentic and genuine manner. You are not looking for a best friend or a future spouse. You are getting to know other people. You are expanding your circle of connections. You are expanding your ability to help them and their ability to help you. That's it! Nothing more. The problem with network-ing is that we often wait until we *need* to network to begin seeking those relationships. This is a bad plan that leads to all of the neg-ative feelings previously mentioned.

Your Network Has the Inside Scoop

Your network knows when someone is leaving his or her depart-ment long before anyone else does. Your network knows when their organization is going to expand and have opportunities. Your network knows about the company and boss who are going to interview you for your promotion. Your network knows about your skills and personality and where you may be a good fit for future opportunities. The information you read on job boards or internal job postings is blanket information that everyone can find out. Networking connections give you inside information. That is, if you have a network!

How to Network Like Miss America (or Mr. Universe)

Networking is not as difficult as it is made out to be. Because there are high expectations around what a relationship may mean in the future to your career, we make the whole experience much more than it should be.

Whenever I hear someone complain about networking, I tell them about Nate. Nate left his job and decided to move to a com-pletely different industry. Not knowing anyone in that field, Nate created a compelling email to send to every successful individual in that industry. He introduced himself, told a little bit about why he was emailing them, and asked for 15 minutes of their time. Nate heard back from 99 percent of those he emailed (his email was quite good!) and secured a job from one of those contacts within 30 days. Networking works if you do it correctly. Let me share some networking tips to get you started.

1. Make sure you begin networking long before you need the contacts. When you have no ulterior motive, the relationship can emerge in a normal, natural manner. Even Carl, the intern in your department who just graduated from college, can tell when you are networking only to help yourself.

2. Be able to speak clearly and concisely about what you do and the work experience you have had. Choose one or two points that you love about your work and keep everything you don't like about your work to yourself. Be positive and don't overwhelm people during the first meeting. It is a polite get-to-know-you and that's it. Remember you can always ask for his or her card or make a link with them later. It is only the *start* of the relationship.

3. If you don't know the person you are speaking with, aim for a 5- to 10-minute conversation and no more. Be brief, be brilliant, and then be gone! During those 5 to 10 minutes, introduce yourself and have one or two questions ready to ask the person you are meeting. Get to know them, show personal interest and be a friend. If you are not good in conversing with others, have some ideas beforehand of what you want to ask.

4. Stay on the topics of work rather than venturing into personal territory. Save those types of discussion points for a later time. Be careful not to talk too much and be sure to ask the individual about him- or herself so that you have a two-way conversation. Stick with your 10-minute rule and politely excuse yourself when the time is up so you have the opportunity to meet other individuals. If the conversation is

engaging and goes longer than 10 minutes, that's fine. Just don't overstay your welcome. Other people want to meet that individual and have a chance to talk with him or her, also. I have seen many trainwreck networking conversations, so be wise and follow this counsel.

5. Never, ever, ever, make connections based on whom you assume is important and who is not. One of the best lessons I can share is that the people you are getting to know now may be the leaders who will hire you tomorrow. Everyone is important in some way or another. Your job is to figure out in what way. The assistant you keep blowing off may be the person who helps you get time with the vice president. Be the person who recognizes the worth in every person you meet.

6. Put the puzzle pieces together. As you have conversations, and listen and learn about people, you are going to find ways that you can connect different people in the room. As you help them, they will want to help you.

7. Follow up with everyone you meet through an email or LinkedIn. Let them know how glad you were to meet them and bring up one point of your conversation. If you made any promises, be sure to follow through. One action that will set you apart from everyone else will be staying in touch through a quick email once every four to six months. Social media has made maintaining a connection a simple task that can be nonintrusive.

Ryan, one of my clients, is phenomenal at doing this. I know that four months won't pass by without hearing from him. He sends me quick emails that say, "I was thinking about you today and wondering how your book was progressing." Or "I saw George today and I was telling him about your podcast. He is in need of your career advice. I hope you are doing well."

These small notes and gestures continually build a relationship and keep us in contact with each other. Every time I get an email from Ryan, I am sure to respond and find out how he is and what is going on with his career. During the past four years that Ryan and I have known each other, we have helped each other immensely career-wise.

If You're Scared

If you dislike approaching people, you are not a great conversationalist, or you despise crowds and networking, let me share a few tips to make networking as painless as possible.

- Have two or three questions ready to ask.
- Say "hello," introduce yourself, ask a question and then listen. Throw out your second question while you gain your composure, listen some more, and then share something about yourself.
- Keep the conversation short. A quick hello and introduction with a few sentences of small talk is not the ideal, but you can always follow up after the meeting.
- Don't have sweaty hands. If necessary, do some type of pre-wipe before you go in for the shake. Sweaty hands gross people out.

If You Get Super, Super Nervous

If you are extremely shy and the idea of talking with a stranger sends you into a panic attack, let me offer three suggestions:

1. If you know who is attending the event, send out a pre-introduction email. Let them know you are attending the same event and hope to meet in person. This helps

break the ice because you have already been introduced (somewhat!).

2. Set a goal to meet two or three people. You need a goal that will force you to step out of your comfort zone and make the introduction.

3. If you *freak out* at the thought of networking, then bring a friend to help carry the conversation and make the introduction. (Make sure your friend knows his or her role in the conversation!) Be sure you take the lead in the conversation introducing both yourself and your friend. You can then take a step back and let the conversation flow from there.

4. If you can't find a friend, haven't made a pre-introduction, and are still scared, then go for the last resort kind of introduction. I call this the "fly-by." For this kind of introduction, you pinpoint the two or three individuals you need to meet and you go for a one-minute introduction with some excuse of why you can't stay, such as, "I am supposed to be meeting someone right now, but I had to be sure to meet you in person before I left." Go through your one-minute introduction, thank the person, and leave. Do the same thing for the other one or two individuals and exit the room. Be sure to follow up with an email.

The "Gold Mine" of Your Network

Your network will provide you help that you may not be able to get in any other way. Your network has experience and education you don't have. Someone in your network has been there and done that and his or her advice can help you leap over barriers you don't want to go through by yourself. When my wife and I decided to create a children's television show, we discovered that one of our friends was already a part of a successful children's show on a major network. He provided invaluable advice that saved us from some expensive mistakes and helped us complete our project quickly. Your network has expertise in different fields. You never know when you may need a lawyer, a contractor, or someone who is an expert in Thai cuisine. Your network may have an expert in that area. I rarely hire someone professionally or personally that another person has not previously recommended. If you are asking your network for help or a favor, be sure to offer up your expertise. Bartering is much better than just asking. When others help me, I always try to help them in some way in return. If I can't help at that moment, I am eager to do so when they ask me for a favor.

Make the List: Who Is Helping You Achieve Your Strategic Career Plan?

Make a list of those who are currently in your network who can help you achieve your plan. Write down as many names as possible. As you are writing them down, ask yourself if this relationship is strong enough to ask for that person's help. If it is, put a star next to that person's name.

Who Is Not in Your Network, but Should Be? How Are You Going to Connect with Him or Her?

The second part of the list will consist of those who are not in your network, but should be. It is important to identify decision makers and opinion leaders you should know and who should know you. Once you have identified these people, it is important to write down how you are going to connect with them. Talk to your boss or other trusted sources for ideas on how you can most appropriately do this.

I can't stress enough the importance of spending the appropriate time and energy to make sure you have the right connections and network. Study after study and also my own experience have shown that the fastest and best way to get a job is through an employee referral. Building a career is never an individual journey. It is a team effort that requires you to have a network.

So fire things up and get working on your network.

CHAPTER

17

Career Plan Step #7: Identify Both Personal and Professional Barriers to Your Success

All the adversity I've had in my life, all my troubles and obstacles, have strengthened me.... You may not realize it when it happens, but a kick in the teeth may be the best thing in the world for you.

—Walt Disney

Kay's boss has been promoted to a new department and she desperately wants his job. Her oldest daughter leaves for college in a year and the extra money would be a welcome addition to help pay for her daughter's tuition. Kay is excellent at her

159

job and is known as one of the most knowledgeable workers in the department. The problem with Kay getting the promotion is that she never earned the certification needed to qualify her for a manager position in her field of work. She regrets not having dedicated the six months required to earn the certification and realizes now that her lack of preparation and planning may have cost her the position.

Jason makes a good living. He has recently been placed on probation because of his angry outbursts and personal attacks directed toward his co-workers. When Jason hears of a pricing mistake one of his employees made, he walks out of his office ready to let him have it. He knows he should choose a different behavior but he doesn't. He heads straight for the employee's cubicle getting angrier with every stride.

Katelyn is stressed out at work and can barely make it through the day. She has been dealing with her stress by overeating and has gained 30 pounds in the last two months. Appearance is important in her Silicon Valley job. Katelyn can't believe she is doing this to herself and that she has limited self-control. Hating herself, she drives to the fast-food drive-thru and orders two hamburgers, fries, and a chocolate milk shake to top it off. She promises herself she will start eating healthily and exercising "tomorrow."

Spencer doesn't like Jennifer. They haven't been able to get along since they started working together three years ago. Every opportunity Spencer gets, he throws Jennifer under the bus. Spencer found out that Jennifer has applied for a position in another department. This promotion would come with a raise and a bigger office. Spencer is friends with the hiring manager, so he decides to make a phone call and ruin any chance Jennifer ever had at getting the promotion.

We have all done things in our careers that we wondered— what were we thinking? How could I have done that? How could

I have sabotaged what I want? On the flip side, sometimes it is another person or the organization we work in that is to blame for our barriers. (In Jennifer's example, Spencer was her barrier to success.) It seems there are barriers that constantly stop us from progressing and reaching our goals. To overcome these barriers, it is important to first recognize what may be holding you back, both internally, as well as externally. Once you have identified the barrier, you can then choose the action to overcome it.

Internal Barriers

We complain about life's hardships and barriers when, in reality, the most fortified ones are those we put up ourselves. It is a sad but very true statement that we are our own worst enemies. The thoughts we think every day and the actions and behaviors we exhibit move us closer to or farther from what we want to accomplish. Years ago, I didn't believe that our internal barriers and perceptions could have such a profound impact on our decisions and potential for success. I couldn't have been more wrong in my thinking.

When I started my doctorate program, I walked into my very first class, sat down, and quickly began comparing myself. So many bright, young students (there weren't any other mid-30-year-olds!) were in the class. The longer I sat there, the more I convinced myself that I was out of my league. I was going to fail. I wasn't smart enough and my idea of going back to school with a wife, four children, and a full-time job was ludicrous. On the first break, I packed my bag, and walked directly to my car, intending to leave. As I sat in the car feeling sorry for myself, I made a decision that has had a lasting impact on the rest of my life. I decided I wasn't going to be the one to determine if I should be there or not, I would give it my all and then I would let my professors make that decision. It was the best thing I ever did, because they never kicked me out! Not only that, I was also able to contribute in class discussions in a unique way because of my corporate experience.

By focusing on my perceived personal inadequacies (negative thinking), I almost dropped out of graduate school. When I chose to give my best effort (positive thinking), I opened the door to future success.

The largest and most difficult internal barrier we face is fear. (See Chapter 3.) It is important to note that fear is the basis for most of the internal barriers we will discuss, so the skill of identifying your fears is key to overcoming the barriers that are holding you back. Remember, it doesn't matter so much what the barrier is; what matters is developing the ability to overcome it.

Internal Barriers to Overcome

Lack of Focus

Your inability to focus on the most important tasks may be one of your internal barriers. You stay so busy all the time that you "major in minor things" and don't spend time and effort on what matters most. By daily focusing on your priorities, you'll be more likely to take the necessary actions that will move you quickly toward your most important goals.

Your Comfort Zone

You are not growing and achieving if you are in your comfort zone. Don't get me wrong when I say I *love* my comfort zone. Who doesn't? Yet, your comfort zone may actually be a pleasant prison that is keeping you from moving forward. Doing what is most UNcomfortable is what takes you as an individual beyond mediocrity and makes you the type of person who can accomplish *hard* things.

Expectations

You have expectations for everything. You have expectations of what should happen on your birthday and how people should treat you at a nice restaurant. You have expectations of your boss, your organization, and those you love. Beware of expectations in your career and life, especially of areas in which you have little to no control. What you expect to happen may not occur or someone may not follow through. Don't let unfulfilled expectations get in the way of your success. Focus instead on the things over which you do have control.

Doubt

Creating a career plan is always a fun activity. The thought of creating your future career and life always gets people motivated. It is when they begin to put those plans into action that problems and barriers begin to show up. This is when doubt makes its appearance. Doubt gets you to question whether or not you can accomplish your plan. Doubt listens to the naysayers. Doubt listens to your fears. If you begin to doubt, the door is open for you to convince yourself the effort and hard work isn't worth it; you weren't going to succeed anyway. (Okay, that sentence was hard to write because it was so negative.) Don't let doubt ruin your plan. Stick with it, believe in yourself, and quiet those doubting voices.

Waiting for Just the "Right" Time

This is my favorite go-to excuse when I want to avoid something. It's much too easy to procrastinate. I convince myself that the timing isn't right, and if I can just get things more organized, more prepared, or if I work on my plan for a bit longer, then I will be ready to move into action. Except that will never happen because the right time is never going to come! The right moment is not in the future; it is now. The right time to work toward getting that promotion, getting the new position, or making those changes is the very moment you think about it. The right time is right now.

External Barriers

The list gets even longer when we move from internal to external barriers. While I have talked about many of these in past chapters, let's bring them out for a quick review. Your external barriers may include:

A lack of qualifications

A lack of experience

A lack of the necessary education

The inability to relocate for a promotion or new job

A bad branding you've created for yourself

A lack of necessary social skills

A negative work environment

Working with all the wrong people

The office politics are not in your favor

A negative office culture

Being in trouble in the past

Co-workers who don't like you

A lack of the right network or connections

The list could go on for another 10 pages but you get the point. The important next step is identifying your own internal and external barriers. If you feel like you can't do this on your own, then find a close friend or loved one and have an open discussion on what he or she perceives are your barriers. This discussion will get your thoughts flowing and hopefully open the floodgates to help you learn more about yourself.

Identify and List the Top Five *Internal* Barriers That Stop You from Achieving Your Goals

1.

2.

3.

4.

5.

Identify and List the Top Five *External* Barriers That Are Keeping You from Succeeding

1.

2.

3.

4.

5.

The Holy Grail of Barrier Busting

Now that you have identified your internal and external barriers and come face to face with the hard truth, it is time to learn how to overcome those barriers. This life-changing three-step process may seem simple, but can make a real impact on your ability to overcome barriers. The first step is to detach yourself from the emotion that each barrier causes. When we come up against these barriers, we can get angry, upset, hurt, or feel rejected. When these emotions surface, it is important to separate the emotions we are feeling from the barrier we are facing.

Todd is a good example of detaching from the emotion. I met Todd while working on a project and immediately knew he was intelligent and a doer. Todd had one flaw, though. He felt like he was never heard in management meetings. After an important meeting, Todd approached me visibly upset because he had been interrupted and passed over before he was able to complete his comments. We discussed why he was being overpowered in these meetings, what he could do about it, and how to detach the angry emotions associated with the problem. His next meeting couldn't have gone better. "I didn't get angry when I was interrupted. I just found another hole in the conversation to insert myself in," Todd reported back. As you implement this three-step process, the emotions may not go away, but you can choose to deal with them differently.

The second step is to change our perception of the barrier. Instead of looking at the barrier as an enemy that is destroying our chances for success, look at the barrier as the *way* to your success. How can this barrier help you, teach you, and prepare you for success? Look through the lens of positivity and see how this barrier is moving you closer to your end goal.

Two departments were combined in a corporate restructuring. They didn't like each other because in the past they had sold competing products to the same customer base. I was brought in to help them overcome these barriers to the success of their combined department. I quickly identified that each department had complementary skills and knowledge. I helped them recognize that by working together, they could quickly increase their success with customers. As they changed their past perceptions, they were able to see the potential benefits of the newly reorganized department and were then able to work together amicably.

The third step is to take action to overcome the barrier. Remember in high school or college when you had a research paper due and all the dread that accompanied the assignment? You knew you should start the paper weeks before it was due, but it seemed overwhelming and you were busy with other class-work. You didn't know where to begin and you figured you had more time tomorrow. Then one or two days before the paper was due, you finally got started and found it wasn't as nearly as big or as difficult as you imagined it would be. The same goes for your barriers. Once you begin to take action to overcome them, they won't seem so ominous and overwhelming. Take one or two significant actions and watch how your perception changes in relation to the barrier. The key is to *start*. By taking just one action, you'll realize that you have the ability to overcome what is stopping you.

Steps to Overcoming Your Barriers

Step One is to identify what negative emotion is connected to the barrier, then to detach from that emotion when confronting the barrier.

Step Two is to change your perception of the barrier. How is this barrier going to help you succeed?

Step Three is to identify the immediate action you are going to face and overcome the barrier.

Write down each of your barriers and the steps you need to take to overcome them.

Example Barrier: Anger

Step One	Detach from feeling hurt that others got the promotion you wanted
Step Two	Maybe I prefer a lower-stress job with less responsibility anyway
Step Three	Take on a small project with a little more responsibility to see whether I like it or not

Your Barrier

Step One

Step Two

Step Three

Your Barrier

Step One

Step Two

Step Three

Your Barrier

Step One

Step Two

Step Three

CHAPTER

18

Career Plan Step #8: Achieving Your Career Plan: The Power of Work

If you are poor, work.... If you are happy, work. Idleness gives room for doubts and fears. If disappointments come, keep right on working. If sorrow overwhelms you, ... work.... When faith falters and reason fails, just work. When dreams are shattered and hope seems dead, work. Work as if your life were in peril. It really is. No matter what ails you, work. Work faithfully.... Work is the greatest remedy available for both mental and physical afflictions.

—Kosaren

A man worked in the U.S. Treasury Department investigating cases in which counterfeit money was involved. He was so good at what he did all he needed was a quick look at a bill to tell whether it was genuine or counterfeit. One evening at a press

169

conference following the breakup of a major counterfeit ring due to this man's work, one of the reporters directed a statement to him: "You must spend a lot of time studying counterfeit bills to recognize them so easily."

His reply was, "No, I don't ever study counterfeit bills. I spend my time studying genuine bills; then the imperfection is easy to recognize."

When we are able to study and plan out the career path we want and then begin to master the art of work, we will clearly see the "imperfections" or the divergent roads that will prevent us from reaching our goals.

Work for Satisfaction and Success

When I was growing up, every Saturday in the Bray household was the same. I would wake up to my sweet mother vacuuming my room around 6:30 A.M. As a teenager, I would have been out until midnight or 1:00 A.M. with my friends the night before so all I wanted to do on a Saturday morning was sleep in. That was not acceptable to my mother and was never going to happen in her house. Saturday was a workday, and next to my cereal bowl I would always find a chore list. This was nothing short of her form of torture; I didn't like her very much on Saturday mornings. But she knew a secret I hadn't learned yet, that there is power in work.

Work is one of the greatest tools you have for creating your own success. I constantly read in business magazines and blogs about those who reached success only to quit everything, in order to relax and "enjoy" the rest of their lives. They worked hard to make money so now they can rest and relax at the beach, have barbecues, buy sports cars, and vacation all over the world. Those articles are written in a way to suggest that the goal of every individual is to finally "make it" and be able to lie by the pool for the next 40 years enjoying success. Don't kid yourself, there are days I would welcome that life with open arms, especially while traveling for work when I'm squished on an airplane between a WWF wrestler and a sweet grandma who has one too many stories she wants to share. But I already know what happens to a life when the focus is on ease rather than industry. I have interviewed enough successful people to understand that the moment the work stops, the heartbreaking stories of unhappiness, boredom, addiction, failed relationships, and other hardships begin.

Work. And work hard!

It Is Better to Work Than Not to Work

Think about it, the passionate man or woman struggling and working hard to build or create something, chases a dream and finally realizes success. Then the realization comes that the joy was in the journey; it wasn't the end result. It is who you become, and what you experience *while* working and creating your career that provides feelings of progression and fulfillment, feelings of satisfaction and success. I believe in most circumstances it is better to work at a job you don't like than to be out of work. Some of the most miserable people I have met are those who have been unable to or have chosen not to work.

What if everyone quit his or her job. What if they were fed up, had enough, and were done with it! Who is going to be there to open the convenience store so I can get my Big Gulp? Who is going to be there to teach our kids math and spelling? Going to a Friday night high school football game isn't going to happen if there is no coach or referee. Our world would be a much different place if people chose not to work every day.

You think you would love not having to go to work but that just isn't true! Even a bad job is better than no job because there can still be personal growth and development. There is always value in hard work. I hear statements from many who have been laid off, fired, or displaced to a different department.

"I miss my job and my friends. I understand now that I was a constant complainer and my behavior probably moved me up the list when they laid people off."

"My job wasn't nearly as bad as I thought at the time. Losing it put everything in perspective."

"When I moved departments, I was so glad to get out of that place. The funny thing is now I spend my breaks and lunches with people from that department."

Don't think of your work as an imposition on your time and something you *have* to do. Look at it instead as an opportunity for you to develop, grow, and advance. If you absolutely hate your job and you are only biding your time until you can make a change, get everything you can out of that position. Learn and master the skill sets that will help you in the future. Take advantage of corporate development, knowledge, and skills acquired from your position as well as networking opportunities. You may look back and be grateful you had that job.

I know because I have been there. I didn't love my first job out of college. (Who does, right?) Everyone else thought I had a perfect job and couldn't believe it when I shared that I wasn't very happy. For the first few years, I was glad just to have a job, so I kept those feelings to myself. Realizing I wanted something different, I decided to prepare myself for the future. I chose to take advantage of every development opportunity my company had to offer. I got my MBA, attended every leadership development class, and did everything I could to prepare myself for the next step. I look back now and love that company for who they helped me become.

Learn to Love the Work You Are Doing

You may hate the job, but you can still love the work. I look back at some of my jobs over the years and while I hated certain aspects of the jobs, there were other aspects I loved: the people, the opportunity to develop skill sets, and the value of seeing and experiencing both positive and negative leadership. Some of those jobs I hated are the very reason I am successful today. If only I could have understood the lesson that the jobs I disliked were developing me for future positions, that insight would have saved me from feelings of discontent. Learn from my mistake and consider how you may be benefitting from the very job you dislike. (At the very least, hopefully you are learning to love the work.) Michelangelo, the virtuoso painter and sculptor, sums up my thoughts when he shared his insight about work, "If people knew how hard I had to work to gain my mastery, it would not seem so wonderful at all."

These last few chapters have covered self-analysis, job analysis, and creating a career plan, all of which will help launch the career you want. We will now switch modes from planning and strategizing to the actual doing. This point in the career plan is where many of my clients freeze. They love planning what career they want and who is going to help them get there. They enjoy diagnosing their job strengths and uncovering the barriers holding them back. But when it is time for the rubber to meet the road and time to get to work, the engines often stall. Nothing great will ever happen by merely planning it; we also have to *make* it happen.

Career Plan Step Eight is a listing of the top five most important things you need to do to achieve your strategic plan. At this point, you know where you want to go, so it is time to get the feet and brain moving to make it happen.

The First Few Steps

As you begin to put the career plan into action, you will have some negative companions the first few steps of the journey. All the fears you have carried and all the barriers that have held you back are going to make an attempt to stop you from the very outset of your journey. I am sending up the warning flag so you are not surprised when they show up. The secret to bypassing them is to focus on the work at hand. Knowing the five most important things you need to do to achieve your plan will ensure that you get those things done first. Your focus will be on the things that will make you successful. So with your career plan in hand, write down the top five things you need to do to achieve your plan.

Don't skip this part and assume that you already know what to do. It may be clear in your mind, but by writing it all down, you can determine if the steps are in the right order and get an idea of the time you will need to complete each step.

For example, if you know you want to get promoted and your company requires an MBA, you are going to need to further your education. So the first step would be to find out if your company reimburses for schooling and start looking for an MBA program that fits your work schedule. The thought of navigating all of this will change when you take the time to write down the first steps you need to take.

Another action item may be the need to enlarge your network. There is a department in your company that you would love to work in, but you don't know the boss. The action item will be to get to know the leader and begin to build a relationship so you can start conversations about possible openings in the future and ask what skills sets and competencies you can be working on right now to make you viable for the position. (The secret is to get the job long before the opening is ever posted!)

Take a moment to identify the steps you need to take.

Top Five Important First Steps to Achieving Your Career Plan and the Deadline for Each Step

1.

2.

3.

4.

5.

Hard work is the secret sauce in creating the career you want. Work will be the key to your success. I often get asked how I earned an MBA and two Ph.D.s. My answer is simple, "I worked." While everyone else watched reality TV at night, I took a class. While many of my friends golfed on Saturdays, I wrote term papers. There were moments I regretted my decision, but I knew if I was going to get where I wanted to be, I needed to make some sacrifices. So I did. I plugged along and worked hard. I was never considered the smartest in the class, never the most eloquent speaker, and I rarely earned the highest grades. But I loved what I was studying and knew it would prepare me for future opportunities, so I kept on working. When things look like they aren't going your way, get to work and things will turn out just fine. Let me close the chapter with one of my favorite Oklahoma sayings, "Go get'er done!" Remember, it's up to you and no one else.

CHAPTER

19

Career Plan Step #9: Return on Investment

We make a living by what we get, but we make a life by what we give.
—Winston Churchill

Percy Ross was known for making and losing fortunes. In his twenties and thirties Ross made and lost two fortunes. In his early forties, Ross started a third venture investing in plastic bag manufacturing and nearly lost everything, but with the help of his wife, Laurian, who sold her expensive furs and jewelry for capital, Ross turned the company around and made millions. In 1969, he sold the firm for $8 million. He took the money and invested in box manufacturing, and also bought General Motors stock. When the big money started coming in, Ross began living the high life. He had five luxury cars in his garage and had a color television installed in his shower. He continued this frivolous spending until he decided he could do more productive things with his money.

Ross decided to write a column in the newspaper called "Thanks a Million," which would be considered a cash giveaway column. Readers would write to Ross asking him for money and the reason they needed it. Ross would make a decision about whom he would give the money to. Ross provided money to readers to fix a leaky roof, help out a farmer, and replace a stolen artificial arm. If the reason was a good one, Ross would send the money or deliver it in person. The readers could forget any financial help if they needed money to pay rent, utility bills, or credit card debts; Ross felt those should be paid by the debtor. His column ran from 1983 to 1999 in more than 800 daily and weekly newspapers. Although known to be a publicity hound, Ross must also have had altruistic motives. He estimated he handed out more than $30 million during the 16-year column run. He stopped the article in 1999 because he had spent a majority of his fortune. To the readers of his column, he wrote: "You have given me so much over the years. In many respects, I'm far richer today than when I started."

As you begin to reach your career goals and attain the positions and income that you have worked so hard for, it is important to determine what you are going to do with your success. Whether your success is defined by knowledge, money, authority, or the influence to create change, you need to make the decision now what you will do with your success and whom you will help. This return on your investment (ROI) is about more than just giving money, it is about giving back in ways that only you can. There is only one you, and your career and personal journey have taught you many skills and information about the specific industries and trades you have worked in. It can be incredibly satisfying to put that knowledge and experience to use in helping others.

Achieving success from the career plan manifests itself in numerous ways. Some will increase their wealth, others will become experts in their field, and some will learn how to use all their experience and knowledge to help others. I am hoping you will have all three. There are a lot of people with money (and many of them have done much to support good causes), but there is only one you who can share and teach what you have learned.

Return on Investment (What Are You Going to Do for Others?)

To guide your thoughts and ideas on how to best give your return on investment, I have included five questions. I am fine with you not immediately writing down an answer. Think about this topic, and when the answer comes and you feel good about it, then write it down. My goal is to get you to think about this right from the beginning so as you progress through the career plan, you can make decisions about your ROI long before you reach the end.

1. How can you give back to your family? (Immediate and extended)
2. How can you give back and use your skills for your work team?
3. How can you give back and use your skills to mentor those who are new to the industry or just starting their careers? How can you make their lives easier and help them avoid some of the pitfalls that you experienced?

4. What can you do for your industry? With your knowledge and success, what can you contribute to make it better?

5. What can you do for the people in your community? In the world?

Don't get overwhelmed by the questions. This is not an Accomplish Everything on the list type of task. This is getting you to see the bigger picture and the possibilities of how you can affect those around you. I encourage you to start small and begin by finding a way to give ROI at least one to two hours a month. You will be amazed not only at how it makes you feel, but also how much you can do and the impact you can make.

I Don't Have Extra Money

"But Dr. Bray, I don't have a lot of money to give at this point."

This ROI isn't only about the money, in fact I would encourage money to be one of the last things you give. It is easy to give money. It is much more difficult to give of yourself. I want you to give your hard-earned knowledge, expertise, advice, and mentoring. Give them something worth more than money. Give them your time and your knowledge.

Here is a great example of giving back with little or no money. Benard Didacus Opiyo is from Uradi Village in Kenya, Africa. In 2008, Benard and his friend George started talking about the horrible educational standards in his village. The poverty level in his region is high and a large percentage of both girls and boys were dropping out of school. Even among those who graduated, only a small fraction of students were making it to the university level. The situation of the girls was dire because of early pregnancies and a long-held cultural perception that girls were not worth spending funds on for an education.

Benard and George knew something had to be done, so they decided to build a school and create a change in their village. In 2010, they founded the Uradi Girls High School with the motto of "molding achievers." They currently educate nearly 100 girls at the school. When the school is fully completed, they expect to educate a total of 360 girls. The goal of all those involved in this village school is to successfully keep students in school no matter what the challenge and help them graduate from university so they can become self-sufficient business people who will then mentor and financially assist other girls. (See http://liveyourlegend.net/.)

With little money, Benard and George did much of the work themselves: they taught the girls, they helped build the school, and they inspired others in the village to help them without pay. They inspired a vision of a better future for the girls in their village.

I could go on with hundreds of examples to inspire you with what is possible, but this is something that only you can decide. Let me give one warning: in the excitement of reaching your goals and everything that goes along with it, be careful not to forget your ROI and your responsibility to give back. Helping others will only make your journey more rewarding.

Interesting Research

As I wrote this chapter, I couldn't help but wonder (and then of course, research) who gave away the most money in 2014. The results were shocking! An article released by the *Chronicle of Philanthropy* laid out the donations made by the 50 most generous Americans in 2014. Let me share the top 10 for the sake of some fun.

Bill Gates	$1.5 billion (Microsoft, in case you have been living under a rock)
Ralph C. Wilson	$1 billion (founder and owner of the Buffalo Bills)
Ted Stanley	$652 million
Jan Koum	$556 million (built Whatsapp and sold it to Facebook)
Sean Parker	$550 million (yes, that's Sean Parker of Napster and Facebook fame)
Nicolas Woodman	$500 million (GoPro guy)
Michael Bloomberg	$462 million (CEO of Bloomberg L.P.)
Rachel Lambert Mellon	$411 million (Philanthropist)
Sergey Brin	$382 million (Creator of Google)
Paul Allen	$298 million (Microsoft)

Your return on investment is the best way to reward yourself before, during, and after you achieve your goals. According to a study published in the *American Review of Public Administration*, helping others while on the job can boost your happiness at work. The study showed that being altruistic not only improves one's well-being at work, it also makes people feel more committed to their work and less likely to quit. Study researcher Donald Moynihan, a professor at the La Follette School of Public Affairs at the University of Wisconsin, said, "Our findings make a simple but profound point about altruism: helping others makes us happier."[1] You get the point—find a way to give back.

---

[1] *Huffington Post*, September 28, 2015.

20

Career Change: Try Before You Buy

My Daughter:	Dad, I'm hungry.
Me:	Let's go home and grab something to eat. I don't have cash.
My Daughter:	Do you have your Costco card? We can go eat there.
Me:	But I told you I don't have cash.
My Daughter:	You don't need cash. You just walk around the aisles and they feed you for free.

Bryant decided on a whim to leave his corporate job and start a consulting business. Despite numerous conversations with family, friends, and work counterparts who urged him to go slow and make a plan, Bryant made the leap and quit his corporate job. Unfortunately, the consulting did not work out like he had hoped and Bryant needed another job to pay the bills and keep his home. He called his past manager and asked for his job back, but the position had already been filled. He asked if there were any other positions he could take, but Bryant's performance before he left was mediocre at best and the company didn't want him back. Bryant was out of work and out of money. He had made two cardinal mistakes: he didn't have a plan and he didn't follow my advice of *try before you buy*.

The stress Bryant went through during that time was immense. For years researchers have been studying the cause and effects of stress. Thomas Holmes and Richard Rahe[1] examined medical records and surveyed over 5,000 patients to determine what causes stress at work. They discovered that changes related to your career are considered some of the most stressful aspects of life. Out of the top 20 stressors individuals deal with in life, Holmes and Rahe found that 3 out of the 20 dealt with career issues. Yes, you read that right! There is a reason that you have wrinkles, can't sleep, are impatient, and carrying around an extra five pounds; it is because of your job! (Blaming and excuse-making is so much fun.) I have learned over the years that changing jobs, if done correctly, can be a smooth road in spite of the stress. Or, if you are unprepared, it can be one of the bumpiest paths you will ever experience, as Bryant learned.

What Is "Try Before You Buy"?

Nearly everything today is a try-before-you-buy scenario. Every time I go to Costco, I get to sample and try the food before I buy it. When I go get yogurt on the weekends (okay, and weekdays), I get to sample that before I buy. Car companies are starting

---

[1] T. H. Holmes and R. H. Rahe, "The Social Readjustment Rating Scale," *Journal of Psychosomatic Research* 11, no. 2 (1967): 213–218.

programs to let potential buyers take the new car home for 24 hours to try it out. I like this concept and find that it fits well with career development and change theories. Jumping from one career or job to another is stressful and full of possible complications, but the try-before-you-buy principle may be just what the doctor ordered before you decide to make a career jump.

Take Prudential, which launched in 2010 a program called CDP, or the Career Development Program, which allows people to stay in their current jobs while doing additional training for a different job. This six months of training is done mostly online and at the candidate's own pace.[2] This program allows the individual to earn the designations required to become a certified life insurance agent and financial adviser. This is just one of many options available. But the try-before-you-buy idea needs to fit your career plan, so let's cover all the information.

By this point in the book, you should have finished your career plan and may be starting to get a feel for what you want to do. You probably have a sense of whether change is on your horizon or if you'll be able to create the career you want in your current organization.

Consider the options of the most common career changes:

1. Changing jobs, but staying in the same organization.
2. Going from one organization to another, but staying in the same field.
3. Going from one organization to another and changing to a completely new line of work.
4. Leaving corporate America to start your own business.

---

[2] Anne Fisher, "Prudential's Secret for Hiring Self-Starters: Try Before You Buy." *Fortune*, September 12, 2012, http://fortune.com/2012/09/12/prudentials-secret-for-hiring-self-starters-try-before-you-buy/.

5. Graduating from school and getting a job. (Welcome to greater stress, my young graduate friends!)

6. Returning to the workforce after a long absence: after raising children, being a caregiver, dealing with a personal illness or that of a loved one, or returning to corporate America after owning your own business, and so forth.

If you have decided to make a change, this chapter is for you! Here's where you can get upfront, to-the-point advice. This chapter is your how-to guide for the three most important steps to ensure a successful career change:

1. Make sure you are changing for the right reason.
2. Gain the information you need to make a good decision.
3. Experience the job before you make a jump.

Buckle up, here we go!

Changing Careers for the Wrong Reason

When you work at an organization for a certain period of time, it becomes your norm. When you decide it is time for a change and you are ready for a promotion or a new job, you need to carefully analyze the reasons you want to leave. One of the biggest mistakes my clients have made is confusing their dislike of the type of work they do with the dislike of their current organization. They are very different things. If you like your career and the work you do and feel competent with your skills, the problem may be with your employer. The issue may arise from the circumstances and environment of your work.

Another reason individuals change for the wrong reason is because they are bored. Generally, after working in a position for four to five years, you are going to get bored. You have been there and done that far too many times. You understand the work, you know how to complete it quickly, and there are very few aspects of the work that can surprise you. The problem is that you may not be learning and progressing, which is a surefire way to get bored. (See Chapter 6 for the solution to this problem.)

One of the biggest reasons people change jobs for the wrong reason is based solely on money. I understand that money is not only important but is essential to our lives. Money is what provides for your home, apartment, car, food, and weekend fun. The temptation to go to certain companies based on their big salaries and benefits can be very attractive. But as my grandpa used to say, "Everything comes with a price." Higher salaries could mean longer work hours, more responsibilities, and a heavier workload. More money could mean more stress, more drama, and working with people you don't enjoy. There is a reason companies pay what they do and your salary could be based on many things, such as your skills, your education, your experience, or what you may have to do or put up with at the new company. You may find that the extra money you made from switching organizations does not make up for the loss of your work and life balance.

Money does not always equate to happiness. I have worked with individuals who made quite a bit more money when switching jobs then discovered after a year or so that the money wasn't worth it so they started the process of switching back. Evaluate what you are leaving (friends, good work environment, good company, and great boss) for what you are gaining.

A last reason you may change jobs for the wrong reason is outside influences or others' expectations. Mom and Dad wanted you to be a manager, not a salesperson. Your spouse wants the benefits that go with the other company you have been interviewing with. Your friends have been promoted or taken new jobs and they are making more money and seemingly having more fun than you. All of these pressures can create a feeling that you need to be making a change as well. I see this while helping Fortune 100 organizations develop their high-potential employees, I recognized that after some of the individuals in each class started to get promoted, others felt the need to get promoted quickly as well. Getting promoted became more important than choosing the right position and the right fit for the individual. Remember this is the job that you have to go to every day. This is the job in which you spend 40-plus hours of your life every week. You will be the one working the job, no one else, so be wise when being influenced by others about what jobs you take and how you expect your career to unfold.

Getting the Right Information

My nephew was a private investigator. Every time we had him over for dinner, he shared stories and experiences from his work. He would talk of late-night observations, following individuals, and hidden cameras like it was the norm for him. Talk about great dinner conversation. One night while discussing his job, he said something that I have repeatedly shared ever since. He said, "When it comes to anything in life, the more information you have, the more power you have, and the more power you have, the better decisions you make." I absolutely agree with his statement. Information is power when it comes to changing careers or changing organizations. Once you have decided to make a change, you need to become your own personal private investigator and learn as much as you can about a prospective career: the responsibilities, the people, and the organization.

Prospective Careers and Jobs

It is difficult to know how day-to-day life looks for certain careers. We look from the outside and perceive jobs from our perspective, but the realities for that job may be completely different. It is up to you to explore your new career path and get the information you need. Here are some tried and true ways to try before you buy. I recommend all of them. Do as many of these as possible.

1. Go on what is called a "vocation vacation." A vocation vacation is when people take an actual paid vacation to go work their dream job for a week or two. You get to experience firsthand what the job entails for one or two full weeks. You can find everything from a veterinarian vacation to working on an emu farm. Take your pick! There are numerous companies you can pay to "test drive" a career that piques your interest. It will give you an insider's view of the job.

   Now don't laugh and think you would never do this. When Chris Macey who works in the oil and gas industry, contemplated a career change, his thoughts turned to animals. Macey put down the funds and spent his vacation working at Schroeder's Den Doggy Daycare in Hillsboro, Oregon. The experience with more than 40 dogs lived up to his dream, but was balanced out by owner-operators Pam and Wayne Pearson who provided a full view of information on all the nuts and bolts (or feed and poop) of running a business. It was an eye-opener for Chris, who started searching for locations to start his own doggy daycare when he returned home. It gave Chris a realistic view of what his dream job would be like. If you are thinking of changing your job, doing a week's worth (or a few days) of on-the-job training which will give you the information you need to make a wise decision.

2. Consider evening and weekend moonlighting. This is the same concept as the vocation vacation, just a different way of going about it. Spend some time in the evenings and on weekends working your future job. You may be surprised at how many companies will let you come in and shadow someone to get a good feel for the job. Search your network for those who already work in the industry. With only a few email requests, I bet you will be able to spend a day or two working your future job. One of my friends' moms loved making soap. In the last decade she has created a phenomenal thriving business that is still growing! She took what she loved, tested it at local farmers' markets and local stores, and found there was a customer base for her product. (You can check her out at www.thesoaplady.net.) I highly recommend her products!

   Try before you buy may mean you'll be putting in some long days to find out if your next job is what you think it will be. Trust me, the sacrifice now will pay dividends in the future.

3. Talk to friends, friends of friends, and their friends. Find individuals who work in your field of interest and ask them for a half hour of their time to tell you about their job. Take them out to lunch or dinner and "vampire" them for information. Ask for both the positives and negatives of their job so you can get the real scoop on a day in the life. As a side benefit you will increase your network! Be sure to be discreet

if you plan on leaving your organization. Word can get out fast and ruin your current job.

4. Take some classes. If your new job requires different training or skills, take a few evening and weekend classes to make sure that you are a good fit. You will meet other students who may already be in the field, as well as teachers who can give you good information about potential jobs. Be wary of signing up for expensive courses or certifications; you can get what you need from the local university or colleges as well as online education platforms.

5. If you know the organization you want to move to, get in touch with as many employees as possible. See if your friends can provide you introductions or use LinkedIn to find and connect with current employees. You will be amazed at how openly current employees will share information about their job and how happy or unhappy they are. Be sure to talk to more than one or two individuals, as you will need a full view of the organization.

6. Consult. If you have an area of expertise and you have always wanted to see if it could become a job, put the word out and consult on a vacation day or evenings and weekends. See if what you have to offer is valuable. Now before you blow that idea off, this was how I started my business. While in graduate school, I got the word out that I wanted to speak about employee excellence in the workplace. A mid-sized company in Oklahoma City didn't have a lot of funds to pay for a speaker for an employee event, so I was hired and the business began to grow from there. Was I an overnight sensation? (Well, maybe in my own head because I had been paid to speak!) No, but I did get to test whether or not I liked speaking and presenting and whether or not the company and people liked what I had to say and found it helpful.

7. Start a side business.

8. Find a try-before-you-buy organization. Like Prudential, which was mentioned earlier in the chapter, there are many organizations that will give you an inside peek into different jobs. This is not currently the norm, but times are changing and you may be pleasantly surprised.

I realize putting these suggestions into action takes time and effort. If you are ready to make a move, it is well worth your time to invest in one or two of the suggestions offered here. They can save you from future problems and issues. Consider this the insurance of career change. I don't know of anyone who invested in gathering information and spent time learning and experiencing a potential job who regretted it. Instead of upping and leaving your job, see if you can get a try-before-you-buy deal to make sure the job will be the right one for you.

CHAPTER

21

Money, Finances, and Your Career Change

The trick is to stop thinking of it as "your" money.

—IRS Auditor

Every day I get up and look through the Forbes list of the richest people in America. If I'm not there, I go to work.

—Robert Orden

Too many people spend money they haven't earned, to buy things they don't want, to impress people they don't like.

—Will Rogers

M oney, bread, bucks, benjamins, bones … it is time to talk about one of the most important aspects of any career. It is the first topic to come up whenever a client shares they want to make a change: the issue of money.

"Money was one of the biggest concerns I had when I decided to change jobs," Kyle told me. Kyle was a serious guy who rarely laughed. He was articulate when we spoke together about career change and was one of the few individuals who knew exactly what he wanted to do. A distinguished man at the age of 42, Kyle did not fit the mold of a college wrestling coach; his brown Chinos and Izod shirt would fit better at the local country club. His stature was more that of a golfer than a wrestler, but wrestling was what Kyle was passionate about. He had left his corporate accounting job to take the position of assistant wrestling coach at one of the top Division II wrestling programs in the United States.

When Kyle left his executive position at the energy company, he approached the head wrestling coach at the local university with the idea of becoming an assistant coach. The coach's immediate reply was, "When can you start?" followed up with, "Unfortunately, we currently have no paid positions." Kyle agreed to the volunteer position while working side jobs using, some of his savings to pay his bills and stay afloat. By the start of the following wrestling season (nearly eight months later), Kyle was still volunteering as an assistant wrestling coach.

In a surprising turn of events, the associate athletic director announced his retirement. The university decided to split his position into two specialized positions within the athletic department. This created a paid position for Kyle while still allowing him time to serve as an assistant coach of the wrestling team. Kyle was ecstatic about the offer and believed the position as associate athletic director would be an excellent opportunity to interact with key individuals on campus, thereby increasing future career opportunities while still doing what he felt passionately about.

Two years into his new position, Kyle realized he was spending the majority of his time working as the associate athletic director, basically doing what he had done at his corporate job, but for less money. His involvement with the wrestling team was decreasing each semester as more director activities consumed his time and energy. After missing two weeks of wrestling practice because of scheduled meetings and other job responsibilities, Kyle spoke to the leadership about the direction of his career:

"I left my previous job so I could pursue something very different, more in line with my goals. Instead, two years later, I am doing exactly what I did before, just not making as much money. I don't know how it happened. I am trying to balance earning a living with working as a wrestling coach."

Money became a major obstacle to Kyle's success during his career transition. He had secured a job he enjoyed, but the money part of the equation was not working out as planned. I would bet $100 (since we are on the topic of money) that most individuals who have experienced a career change have dealt with money problems. Having a financial plan and knowing your options before you make a change is the best way to move past this major money barrier in a single bound.

Have a Financial Escape Plan

If you are wanting to make a career change, it is time to be strategic and devise your financial escape plan. (I have visions of Red and Andy from *The Shawshank Redemption* planning their escape. Pull out your fork and let's start digging out of this prison!) The following is key information you need to know when developing your plan.

If you are planning on moving to another organization, you need to have three to six months of salary socked away somewhere safe. I always recommend securing a new job before quitting your current job, but if you can't stay at your current place of employment, realize the average time it takes to secure a new job is three months. Warning: You don't want to experience the stress of trying to acquire a job knowing you have only one month before your funds run out. It causes desperation and potential employers can smell it a mile away.

If you are planning on starting a business, I encourage you to save up 8 to 12 months of pay. The cost of starting a business on top of the day-to-day expenses is going to cost more than you think. I already know what you are saying to yourself, "Dr. Bray, that would take me two years to save up eight months of salary and I can't wait that long." "Not true" is my response. There are lots of ways to earn money in addition to your current salary. The important thing is for you to be able to focus on your new job or your new business. If you are stressing out about money, losing your hair (both men and women do when they are stressed out!), and trying to scrape by month to month, you are in for a terrifying ride. It is worth it to plan, prepare, and research, then move forward in a way that increases your chances for success. I know, I know … *Entrepreneur*, *Fast Company*, and other business magazines get you excited to start your own business. Their articles spotlight those who have been successful by maxing out their credit cards and mortgaging their homes to launch their venture. Doesn't it seem like all of the entrepreneurs spotlighted in those magazines make millions only one year later? Trust me on this one; the world is much tougher and more brutal than is represented in those articles. Preparation, planning, and knowledge will serve you well and improve your chances for success. Have a plan and have a stash of cash. If these preparations delay you a year, it will be worth every penny to wait.

Plan out the approximate amount of money you will need for your career change and how long the funds will need to last.

I need $ _____ to last me _____ months.

How You Can Earn the Exit?

Once you have a plan for your new career, it is time to earn your exit. Open an account at a local bank or slice a hole in your mattress to have a place to stash the money you need to make your exit. From your plan, you know exactly how much money you need before you can sing, *"Take this job and shove it. I ain't workin' here no more."* (Really, is there any better way to quit a job than to sing that anthem as you walk out the door?) Now it is time to figure out how you are going to earn the money needed to make the change. Here are some suggestions to speed up your exit.

Most individuals cut back on their expenses so they can begin saving toward their six-month recommended salary stash. I agree with this method, but we can put some turbo into that savings plan. While not getting your $5 cup of coffee is going to help you (I know you will be grumpy and tired without it, but you will survive), you can also move to the earning side of the equation and get yourself another stream of income. Get yourself a side hustle (a small job on the side), some freelance work on the weekend, or maybe some extra hours or an additional project at work. This means you will have less free "me" time, but it will add up and will help you exit faster. When you reduce your expenses and also earn more money, the time it takes to reach your exit number will be cut in half. It is worth the sacrifice to do both. If you don't think so or you are not willing to do the extra work, you really didn't want a career change in the first place and I just spared you from a dose of failure.

There are lots of ways to earn extra money. You just need to decide what works best for you. Two options many of my clients have used are flexjobs.com and snagajob.com. Both offer telecommuting, part-time professional jobs. You can also go to any of the job search websites and enter in telecommute or part-time and lots of options will show up. (Also search the term *virtual*.) Some of my clients have consulted and some have even cleaned out their homes and had a garage sale. (After a client had so much success doing this, my own family had a big spring cleaning and held a garage sale that made nearly $1,000.) Whether you need $20,000 or $100,000 in your career change stash, these are some ideas of quick ways to earn it. Remember, this is not for the long term—you are doing this to move to the next step in your career, so go crazy and earn as quickly as you can.

Warning: Be sure you don't break any work agreements or contracts with your current organization. The last thing you want to experience is being fired for having a side job. I recommend all extra earning activities be after hours or on the weekend. (That way you have no conflict of interest.)

Find an Individual to Keep You Accountable

Nothing is more fun than sharing a victory or success with a friend. You are more likely to be successful if you have someone who will keep you accountable. So find a friend or loved one, share your plan, and ask if he or she will help keep you accountable and on track while you work through your career transition. If you don't have any friends or loved ones, then hire a career coach. (Catch the sarcasm?) Having someone to keep you accountable is invaluable during your career change.

Back to Kyle

Six months after our initial interview, Kyle appeared to be much happier. In response to my question of how he was doing, he remarked with excitement that our first discussion "woke him up" to the original reasons he had left his corporate job. He had since spoken with senior-level administrators at the university and expressed concern about his current position. He indicated his desire for a position that would allow him to balance his time with the wrestling program while still managing the athletic department. The administration was very accommodating and changes to his responsibilities were already beginning to take place.

The more prepared you are financially before making a change, the less stressful the experience is going to be. By finding ways to increase your income while cutting your expenses, you can quickly reach the monetary goal you have set for yourself in order to make your grand exit.

22

When Everything Goes Wrong

Nothing either good or bad, but thinking makes it so.

—Shakespeare

It was the eleventh draft of my dissertation. I had invested hundreds of hours of work, blood, sweat, and tears into what I considered my masterpiece. My family had made sacrifices for my schooling and writing for years. I could finally see the light at the end of the tunnel and began to anticipate some free Saturdays filled with fun! The dissertation was completed and I was ready to move on with my life. After eight years of classes, research, writing, and interviewing employees in corporate America, I had 253 pages of brilliance! I was ready to defend my dissertation.

With only a few weeks left to make final preparations for my defense and graduation, I had to get everything done quickly. I pushed the *Send* button, forwarding my dissertation to my chairperson, then went to bed with a sigh of relief.

The next evening I received an email from my chairperson (a very tough, but brilliant professor and writer) with a subject line that read: "A few changes."

I opened the email to find what I considered to be an ocean of red corrections. In fact, I think there was more red than black in the document. I was horrified. I could feel the anger and devastation welling up. How could she do this to me? All I could do was just stare at my masterpiece, now bludgeoned with red like something out of a horror movie. I felt like I had been punched in the stomach. The moment was literally more than I could bear. It would likely mean an additional six months before I could graduate. I didn't know if I had it in me to go two or three more rounds of researching, interviewing, writing, and sacrificing. I wanted to quit. In fact, I was going to quit. Nothing was worth this torture. So I closed my computer and walked away, not knowing when I would pick it back up again. I couldn't even face it. (Fortunately, my wife wouldn't let me quit, but she waited a few days for me to calm down to inform me.)

There will come a day when everything goes wrong, when things don't work out, when you fail, when people turn against you, or even worse, when you turn against yourself. It is in those moments that you want nothing more than to quit, to hide, and to take a break from the world. The emotions that accompany these moments are hard to forget. We feel anger, frustration, confusion, and sometimes, even depression. We come face to face with our fears in a way we rarely do. Unfortunately, all of us at some point in our lives will experience events that knock our feet right out from under us and make us wonder if we can get up again. Getting through these difficult times can seem overwhelming.

The information in this chapter is designed to help you handle the tough times ahead as you develop your career. Here are seven life tools designed to help you survive and even thrive in times of adversity. I hope they will help you when you need it most.

Seven Life Tools to Get You Through Difficult Times

1. Adjust Your Perceptions

Perception is the way that we look at our problems. It is how we understand and interpret the events that happen in our lives. Our perceptions determine our attitude and our approach to solving our problems. Our perceptions can be positive and provide us with joy and happiness or our perceptions can be negative and depressing. It's important to understand that our perceptions are completely within our control. We can choose to see events as positive or negative, which in turn determine our emotions, behaviors, and reactions to those events. It is a shocking concept, but when we learn to put a positive spin on our perceptions of life's events, we take the first step to overcoming hardships and obstacles.

I was sitting in a meeting with a leadership group of a midsized organization. The company was growing and numbers were good but there had been some quality issues surrounding one of the products. As the issues were discussed, things got heated and the president of the division lashed out at two of the vice presidents—criticizing decisions they had made. It was a tough meeting and after it was over, I went to check on the two vice presidents. One of the vice presidents was extremely distraught. He felt he had been treated unfairly and had been accused of making decisions that were not his alone to make. He was visibly angry and protested about how he had been treated.

As I approached the second vice president, I noticed him on his computer. When I asked how he was doing, he responded that he was "fine." He could tell I looked shocked by his response. He continued, "He isn't mad at me. He is mad at the situation. Things will blow over and we'll deal with the problem. This isn't the end of the world. The president wants to be successful and it was upsetting to him when things didn't go as planned." That was a great lesson for me. The second vice president's perception gave him a very different outlook on the experience. His positive perception gave him the power to choose a better reaction. I was in awe of how he handled the situation.

Most of us give in to our initial human reactions and emotions when things go wrong. By learning how to control our perceptions of events and people, we can automatically control our actions and behaviors.

2. Control Your Emotions

As we progress into adulthood, our brains continue to grow and change. The executive function of our brain, which is found in the pre-frontal cortex, helps us make good decisions: decisions that can necessarily override our emotions. When something goes wrong or someone treats us badly, we have an automatic emotional reaction to the situation. We want to strike back in anger or we feel hurt and want to scream or cry. In most of these situations, the best action is to control our emotions (because we will never get rid of them) and to control the negative behaviors that often result from these emotions. Choose to remain calm and collected. That's easy to say while you sit in your comfortable chair reading this book but very difficult to do in the moment. Like riding a bike, learning a new language, or mastering cooking, it is a learned skill. With practice, you can master the art of controlling your emotions. Even though it would be easier to let our emotions rule the roost, incredible outcomes can occur when you elevate yourself and choose to listen to your brain and not just your emotions.

3. Focus on What You Can Control

When life or your career takes a difficult turn, that is the time to focus on what you can control versus what you cannot control. Wisdom lies in understanding the difference between the two. Whenever things are going wrong, take a seat and write a list of the controllables and the uncontrollables. Next, cross off the uncontrollables. Let them go and don't give them the time of day. Look instead at what you *can* control and begin to make decisions about what you are going to do for each of those areas to improve them even more.

4. Don't Compare

This is one of the most deadly habits. When things go wrong in life, one of the first things we do as humans is to compare ourselves to others.

"I work much harder than Danny, and he's the one who gets the promotion!"

"Why don't I get the good job?"

"Why can't I live in that type of neighborhood, or drive that type of car? I'm tired of not being able to afford things like the Joneses."

The cancer of comparison causes you to look at the best in everyone else and compare it to your worst. I consider this self-torture because you will never come out ahead. When you compare, you can't see reality. In the midst of life's difficulties, choose to see yourself as one who is continually striving to improve rather than comparing yourself to others. Happiness and fulfillment come as you work on being the best "*you*," not in trying to be better than another person. Years ago, when I struggled with comparing myself to others, a good friend told me "Do you, Chris. Just focus on doing you, not anyone else." (Which translated means: "Be you. Just focus on being you.") That is when you will be successful and do great things.

5. Don't Allow Self-Pity

When times are especially tough and we feel misunderstood, abandoned, and unable to deal with the situation at hand, we fall into the trap of self-pity. One man said, "Hell is being frozen in self-pity." In those moments, it is easy to indulge in feeling sorry for ourselves. It feels so good to wrap ourselves in a blanket of "I have been wronged." One of my daughters had been crying for what seemed to be a long time. When I asked her why she was crying, she responded, "Because it feels really good." Yes, for a moment, self-pity may feel good but like quicksand, self-pity will draw you in until it is too late to get out and proactively deal with your situation.

I learned one of the best ways to deal with this emotion. While watching a talk show, the host interviewed a guest who had been severely burned over 90 percent of her body. Once a very attractive woman, she was now a shell of her former self. Despite nearly 30 surgeries, her skin still carried the effects of the burns. When asked how she coped, the woman gave a remarkable answer on how she keeps going day after day. The young woman responded, "I let myself cry and feel sorry for myself for 15 minutes every day. Then I get on with my life until tomorrow comes and I can feel sorry for myself for another 15 minutes." That's absolutely brilliant!

6. Choose to Act and Not Be Acted Upon

Deciding to take action instead of being paralyzed by adversity and trials is the true mark of courage and greatness. Here's an important lesson from ancient Greece. Several hundred Spartans were holding the narrow pass at Thermopylae against the Persians who had set out to conquer all of Greece. The Persians came by the thousands to attack. They urged the Spartans to surrender. Then hoping to intimidate them further, the Persians sent emissaries to the Spartans, saying they had so many archers in their army they could darken the sky with their arrows. Against overwhelming odds, the Spartans responded, "So much the better. We shall fight in the shade." That incredible display of courage was a great example of choosing action rather than shrinking or surrendering when everything goes wrong. I doubt all of the Spartans were excited to "fight in the shade," but they acted like they were. And that is what you need to do. In times of difficulty, stand up and act like you want, instead of doing what you feel. This is an amazing concept that will change your life if you follow it. Let me say it one more time: stand up and act like you want instead of doing what you feel.

7. Have Grace Under Pressure

Recently, a neighbor of mine lost his 20-year-old daughter in a devastating accident. She had recently returned from spending 18 months in another country and had been home for only a couple of months. Her death was a shock to everyone who knew her. She was a happy, accomplished, and kind individual. She had been in our home only weeks before babysitting our children for a few days while my wife and I were on vacation. It was heartbreaking. When we went to visit my friend and his wife to offer our support and condolences, they greeted us warmly in their home with love and cheerfulness. I told my wife as we left that I was sure they were still suffering from shock—surely no one could be in that peaceful a state after losing their daughter. But as I watched them over the next few weeks, they continued to exude grace even in their tragic circumstance. I am sure in their quiet moments alone they broke down, wondering how they could continue on without their daughter and wondering if the heartache would ever go away. But when others were around, they chose to celebrate the life she had lived instead of remembering her in sadness and grief.

I have thought deeply about this and wondered how I would handle such a tragedy in my own life. Based on their example, I have come to believe that grace under pressure is necessary not only for our own benefit but also because others are watching us to see an example of how to cope with their own struggles. "Every time we navigate safely through [our hardships], there are other ships that are lost which can find their way because of our steady light of handling obstacles and hardships with grace and peace." (Thank you, Neal A. Maxwell.)

Can you imagine what type of person you would be if you were able to master all seven of these characteristics and traits! Highlight the ones that strike a chord with you and learn to master them. These life tools are ready for you to use when needed to help you get through some of life's tougher moments. I hope this chapter helps. I know it will because these principles have worked for me.

My Dissertation: The Rest of the Story. After receiving that email, which was overflowing with needed corrections for my dissertation, I pouted and felt bad for myself for three days. Then I determined to take my own advice and began to implement the Seven Life Tools to Get You Through Difficult Times (I hadn't named them that yet, but I understood the principles even then.)

Tool One—Adjust your Perceptions: I decided to look at the situation from a long-term perspective. I had worked for many years to get to this point. Was it wise to quit just six months from the finish line?

Tool Two—Control your Emotions: I called my chairperson and shared how devastated I was and how I felt my hard work was not paying off. (I said this instead of telling her I disliked her more than the flu.)

Tool Six—Choose to Act and Not Be Acted Upon: I shared with her that I appreciated her hard work and the effort she was making to improve my dissertation. I told her that I wanted to be just as successful as she wanted me to be.

Tool Seven—Have Grace Under Pressure: I asked her for advice on how to proceed. I asked for help walking through the dissertation so I could fix what needed to be corrected.

My chairperson responded with a shocking statement: "Chris, you are so close. We are to the tweaking stage now where we are 'shining and refining' your work!" Thankfully, I was able to make all the corrections, do the work my professor suggested, and still graduate on time. I was able to do that because I *chose* to put the tools into action. Give it a try and you will be amazed at what you can do.

RECAP:

1. Adjust your perceptions.
2. Control your emotions.
3. Focus on what you can control.
4. Don't compare.
5. Don't allow self-pity.
6. Choose to act and not be acted upon.
7. Have grace under pressure.

23

Start Doing: Take Focused, Smart Actions

"You can discover more about a person in an hour of play than in a year of conversation."

—Attributed to Plato

I t is go time. You have put in some serious work and have everything you need to move forward. So climb up that high dive, take a good look at where you currently stand, and get ready to jump. It may be a little scary, but you can do it. By reading this book and answering the questions as they pertain to you, you are prepared to begin achieving your goals.

The first few steps of *doing* are always the most difficult, but after a few days of action, you'll hit your stride. There is nothing that feels better and motivates you more than moving toward your goals. Action beats intention any day. When you begin to choose actions and behaviors that create the results you want, you are also creating the life you want. It isn't rocket science; it is understanding that if you don't do anything, you won't get anything. Things only change if you take some action. It's hard to get a job if you don't put in a resume. It's hard to return to school if you don't put in an application. It's hard to find someone to date if you don't put yourself out there. One of the laws of life is that action creates results. So let's move from analyzing, strategizing, and planning to real-life action, progression, and accomplishment.

It Is Up to You

If you really want to create your Best Job Ever!, then you are going to have to put some effort and time into it. You have to move past excuses, overcome your life-long ruts, and hold yourself accountable for personally creating the life and career you want. This is not just motivational speak; it is realizing that if you are going to become the person you want to be, *you* have to be responsible for the day-to-day choices. This is the moment to stand up and decide that you are going to do what it takes. No matter the barriers, the naysayers and everything negative your brain can come up with, you can make the decision to behave in a way that is best for you in the long term. You can't spend the rest of your life giving in to the worst part of you. Let the best part of you take the steering wheel from here on out.

Results Matter

From this point on in your career journey, you are going to start measuring your life according to your results. You are going to start keeping score with yourself. What did you do today that moved you closer to your goals? Forget what you *hope* will happen or what you *intend* to do. When you start to see results, you will know you are progressing. That is reality. At work, you are measured by results. In any sport, you are measured by results. In school, our kids are measured by results. That is how life works. That is reality. So start recognizing the rules for your life.

It's Better to Try and Fail

While studying journals and interview transcripts of patients who knew they were dying in the near future, nearly every person wished that he or she had done things, that for one reason or another, they had chosen not to do. Opportunities had come but were missed perhaps because of fear, insecurity, the possibility of failure, or just not knowing how. What caught me off guard was that nearly all of these patients, at the end of their lives, weren't concerned about whether or not the opportunity would have turned out the way they wanted—whether they would have succeeded or failed—they only wished they would have *tried!* Did you catch that? The results didn't matter to them.

That has made a lasting impression on me. As William F. O'Brien's poem title states, "it is better to try and fail than never to try at all." Sounds like a cliché, but that mentality is one I have always tried to teach my children. The outcome is never as important as the effort, because one day your outcome will match your effort and you will amaze yourself with what you've accomplished and what you've become.

Use the Tools and Act to Make a Difference

If there is one thing I love about my job, it is when I get to witness people amaze themselves. I watch for it every day—the amazing things people do that positively affect companies, industries, communities, and perhaps most importantly, another person. They are inspiring because most of these individuals are no different from you and me, only they decided to act differently. Like Max Sidorov, a person you most likely have never heard of—but you may recognize one of his actions in which the outcome amazed even himself.

Karen Klein was on a school bus with a slew of middle school kids. The 68-year-old bus monitor earned $15,600 a year for ensuring the safety of the children as they made their way home each day after school. Her job responsibilities included protecting the kids from physical or verbal abuse. Unfortunately, the kids didn't do the same for Karen. Then one day on the bus, one of the students decided to videotape what Karen's job was really like. When the video went viral, it horrified the nation and caused an international outrage. The videotape caught students taunting and making fun of Karen with a stream of profanity, insults, and comments about her weight and her family. They told her they wanted to come to her home and steal from her. Another boy told her that she didn't have any family because "they had all killed themselves because they didn't want to be near her." (Little did that boy know that Karen's oldest son had committed suicide 10 years earlier.) The comment caused Karen to begin crying, but the kids didn't stop there.

The kids jabbed at her arm with a book and continued their mocking. When you watch the video, it is hard to believe anyone could be so calloused and hurtful. As the bullying continued, Klein told the children, "I am a person, too. I shouldn't be treated this way." For Karen, this was a time when everything was going wrong.

The local news broke the story. It was picked up by international news agencies within hours. The outcry for the boys' punishment was immediate and local authorities approached Karen to see if she wanted to press charges against the boys. The first of two amazing things happened: Karen decided to not push for criminal charges against the boys, but requested that they only be punished.

"They are not all bad boys," she said to the local news. She only wanted to "make sure that they never do this again, to anybody."

After the story was publicized, a second amazing thing happened: someone chose to act on what he witnessed rather than just watch. (I will be the first to admit when I learned about the story I immediately watched the video, felt bad, decided to talk to my kids about the story that night and then went back to my normal life.) But Max Sidorov from Toronto, Canada, did more. He heard the story and decided to take 15 minutes (*yes, 15 minutes*) to set up a fundraiser for Karen on the Indiegogo website so that he could help out, even if only in some small way, to get her away from that negative environment. He thought maybe a trip would be a nice thing for her. The fundraiser brought in more than $700,000 dollars and allowed Karen to retire. The action of one man for 15 minutes had a lasting effect on another individual's life.

You may be wondering: why the 15-minute Max Sidorov story? There are two reasons: first, Karen was an incredible example and amazed the nation (and perhaps herself) by exhibiting the Seven Life Tools to Get Through Difficult Times (see Chapter 22). Second, the story shows that small actions can have dramatic results in life. Likewise, you can have an extraordinary effect on your career by taking small action steps, especially if done consistently over time. Even if it is only 15 minutes. I have witnessed this firsthand. Fifteen minutes a day devoted to your career or to improving your life can have monumental results when added up over a month, six months, or a year. The power of compounding occurs! Whether the action is large or small, it always has an effect. Now is the best time to pull the trigger. Begin now because nothing will change in your life or in anyone else's life if you don't choose to act.

Be Patient with Change

The problem with change is that you want the results all at once. (Me, too!) You have watched one too many sitcoms in which everything gets resolved by the end of the show. Change in real life requires more time and is often a difficult and a hard road to walk. It is more about gaining momentum and moving forward than about how long the process takes.

No Excuses!

"It is too hard . . . . I'm too tired . . . . I can't." My children learned early on that comments like these were going to earn them a one-way ticket to finishing what they thought was too hard. If you think something is hard, that is the very reason you should do it. You have an invaluable lesson around the corner for you to learn. I have worked with individuals who struggled just to make it to my office. One of my clients, Melinda, will help you reset your perception of your life. Melinda is one of the coolest people I know and a phenomenal person to work with. She is witty, hardworking, and a powerhouse. She loves music, concerts, and men (although not in that order, she told me). Melinda has one small issue: half of her body is twisted such that she can barely walk. With her typical positive attitude she told me, "just wait until after my 15 surgeries, I will grow five inches and walk like Heidi Klum."

I have watched her go through half of those painful surgeries and only a few times have I ever heard her say it hurts. She is a realist, but she also has things she wants to do and a certain type of life she wants to live, and her issues are not going to hold her back. I never hear her say, "I can't" or "it is too hard." She keeps moving forward, progressing and doing amazing things in spite of her limitations. Her positive can-do attitude makes all the difference in the world. So before you make the excuses and let your issues hold you back, think of Melinda's inspiring example.

Safety or the Storm?

In life, there are many different types of people. There are some who like to live life safely, do what they can to not rock the boat and live as stress-free a life as possible. When life begins to look scary or uncertain, they have a difficult time. On the other side of the spectrum are those who are considered more risk takers. They enjoy the storms of life. They like to take chances, be stretched, and experience all that life has to offer. They have little to no fear of failure.

In the past, as you have faced uncertainty and change, which end of the spectrum have you been on? If you are going to make some changes in your life, you have to realize you may be giving up your safety anchor for a bit of a rougher ride in the storm. That's okay, just be aware of the difference between staying in the harbor and being out in the storm.

You Are Prepared to Succeed.

As you have worked your way through this book and deliberately answered the questions and applied the knowledge, you have gained greater self-awareness and a new perspective that will begin to Revolutionize Your Life. You've been able to Rethink Your Career: you now know there is no perfect job but you can improve aspects of the one you currently have. Or, if you choose to find a new job instead, you know what to look for to ensure that it will be personally fulfilling. You are now more aware of your personal priorities because you have Redefined What *Rich* means to you.

You now have a strategic plan to move forward in creating your Best Job Ever!

Just Do It Already!

We have had enough talk. Now is the time for you to go and accomplish. Bless the world with your talents, abilities, and incredible mind. Make a difference in what you do and for the people with whom you interact. The secret is to take action every single day to get the momentum moving you toward your dream. This requires only one assignment: each day, write down what action you are going to take that day to achieve your goal. You will thank me later—especially if you keep at it for more than 30 days.

Remember that *doing* is the most important part of getting your Best Job Ever! Your daily actions are what will move you closer and closer to what you want from your life and your career. If sometime in your journey toward your Best Job Ever you feel like you have stalled and things are not going well, the first thing you need to do is *take some action!* I can promise that there will be difficult times ahead, but anytime you do anything worthwhile it is going to be hard.

You now have the tools you need to succeed. Believe in yourself and move forward with confidence.

I wish you all the best in your journey.

Dr. C.K. Bray

Index

A

Action, 211–218
  avoiding excuses, 216–217
  being proactive, 44,
    206–207
  first steps of "doing,"
    211–212, 218
  opportunity and,
    213
  overcoming fear of change,
    31–32
  patience and, 216
  for results, 212–213
  risk taking for, 217–218
  Seven Life Tools to Get You
    Through Difficult
    Times for, 213–216
    (*See also* Seven Life
    Tools to Get You
    Through Difficult
    Times)
Adjust Your Perception
    (Tool 1), 203–204
Altruism, 177–182

*American Review of Public
    Administration*, 182
Angelou, Maya, 114
Anger, detaching from, 168
Apple, 119–121
Assessment
  of current career, 91–93
  for determining career
    interest, 41–44, 62,
    63–64
  standing out and, 129–130
  of strengths, 122–123

B

Barriers, 159–168
  external, 164–165
  internal, 161–164
  overcoming, 165–168
  overview, 159–161
Behavior, motivation and,
    143–147
Best Job Ever, 1–9
  defining, 93–100
  expectations for, 1–6

Best Job Ever (*continued*)
  secret of, 6–9
  See also Action; Boredom;
      Career change; Career
      Plan; Compensation;
      Current Job; Fear of
      change; "Rich"; Seven
      Tools to Get You
      Through Difficult
      Times; Try-before-
      you-buy scenario
Big "Why?," The (Career
      Plan Step 5), 143–147
Boredom, 53–64
  causes of, 55–58
  changing careers/jobs and,
      187
  finding meaning outside
      work environment,
      59–61
  making change and, 63–64
  new experiences for
      overcoming, 58–59
  promotion or department
      change in response to,
      61–63
  realistic expectations and,
      55
  symptoms of, 53–55, 56–58
Bosses, dissatisfaction with,
      13–15
Bray, CK, 42

British Psychology Society, 58
Budgeting, for career change,
      193–199

C
Career, boredom with.
      See Boredom
Career change, 37–45
  for Best Job Ever, 1–9,
      93–100
  identifying reasons for,
      186–188
  initiating, 63–64
  job search research for,
      40–41
  making choice and taking
      action for, 44
  overcoming boredom,
      53–64
  overcoming confusion
      about, 37–39
  personal assessment for,
      41–44
  power of change, 77–84
  progressing toward, 6–9
  within same company,
      61–63, 79, 81
  seeking information about,
      40–41, 62, 188–189
  See also Action; Boredom;
      Career Plan;
      Compensation; Current
      job; Fear of change;

"Rich"; Seven Life
Tools to Get You
Through Difficult
Times; Try-before-
you-buy scenario
Career Development
Program (Prudential),
185
Career fear. *See* Fear of
change
Career Plan
The Big "Why?" (step 5),
143–147
Discover Your Strengths
(step 2), 119–126
goal setting for, 85–100
Identify Both Personal and
Professional Barriers to
Your Success (step 7),
159–168
One-, Three-, and
Five-Year Plan (step 4),
133–141, 147
The Power of Work
(step 8), 169–175
Return on Investment
(step 9), 177–182
What Is Your Job? (step 1),
113–117, 125
What Makes You Awesome
at Work? (step 3),
127–132

Your Community (step 6),
149–158
Challenge, seeking, 58–59
Choice, for career change, 44,
82–83
Choose to Act and Not Be
Acted Upon (Tool 6),
206–207
Chronicle of Philanthropy,
181–182
Comfort zone, as barrier,
162–163
Company employment,
planning for,
136–137
Comparison, avoiding,
205–206
Compensation, 193–199
accountability and
planning, 198
changing careers for, 187
feeling rich and, 69,
72–74
financial escape plan and,
195–196
overview, 193–195
planning and, 138–139
savings and career change,
197–198
Consulting, 191
Contacts, making.
See Networking

Contingency plans, 201–209
  adjusting perception,
      203–204
  avoiding comparison,
      205–206
  avoiding self-pity, 206
  being proactive, 206–207
  controlling emotion,
      204–205
  focusing on controllable
      issues, 205
  handling pressure with
      grace, 207–208
  preparing for difficulty,
      201–203
Control Your Emotions
      (Tool 2), 204–205
Costco, 19
Co-workers, frustration with,
      18–19
Csikszentmihalyi, Mihaly, 58
Current job
  advantages of working while
      seeking employment,
      101–105, 171–173
  best aspects of, 105–107,
      111
  changing aspects of, 110
  job responsibilities of,
      113–117, 125
  negotiable aspects of,
      109–110, 112

try-before-you-buy
      scenario, 183–192
  worst aspects of, 108–109,
      111

D
Department change, boredom
      and, 61–63
"Despite," 31–32
DiSC (personality test),
      123
Discover Your Strengths
      (Career Plan Step 2),
      119–126
Dissatisfaction, with job.
      See Job satisfaction
Don't Allow Self-Pity
      (Tool 5), 206
Don't Compare (Tool 4),
      205–206
Doubt, as barrier, 163
DrCKBray.com, 42
Dream job, 1–9
  defining, 93–100
  expectations for, 1–6
  secret of, 6–9

E
Emotion
  controlling, 204–205
  detaching from, 166–168
  feelings about being rich,
      69–71

Excellence, 127–132
  feedback about, 129–130
  importance of, 129
  mastering skills for,
      130–131
  overview, 127–128
  promoting, 131–132
Excuses
  reasons for, 48–49
  results and problems of,
      49–52
  types of, 47–48
Expectations
  as barrier, 163
  career boredom and, 55
External barriers
  identifying and listing, 165
  overcoming, 165–168
  types of, 164–165
  See also Barriers
External influence, career
      change due to, 187–188

F
Failure, trying and, 213
Fear of change, 23–35
  identifying fear, 28–30
  making excuses and, 47–52
  overcoming fear, 32–34
  overview, 23–25
  reaction to, 26–28
  symptoms of, 25, 26
    taking action in spite of
        fear, 31–32
    understanding fear, 30–31
Feedback
  to assess strengths, 123
  excellence and, 129–130
Fight-or-flight response,
      27–28
Financial issues.
      See Compensation
Flexibility, changing careers
      and, 80–81
Flexjobs.com, 197
"Fly-by," 156
Focus
  Focus on What You Can
      Control (Tool 3), 205
  lack of, 162
  need for, 205

G
Gallup, 12, 19, 121
Goal setting, 85–100
  assessing current career for,
      91–93
  career strategy and,
      87–91
  defining Best Ever career
      for, 93–100
  one-, three-, and five-year
      plans, 133–141, 147
  overview, 85–87

Goodson, Woody, 106

Grace, under pressure, 207–208

H

"Hackathons," 120

Have Grace Under Pressure (Tool 7), 207–208

Helplessness, feelings of, 78–79

"High-spider-fearfuls," 33

Hobby, career *versus*, 104

Holmes, Thomas, 184

I

Identify Both Personal and Professional Barriers to Your Success (Career Plan Step 7), 159–168

"I don't know what to do" problem, of career development. *See* Career change

Information gathering, for career change, 40–41, 62, 188–189

Internal barriers

identifying and listing, 165

overcoming, 165–168

overview, 161–162

types of, 162–164

See also Barriers

Internal politics, 15–17

Introductions, 156. *See also* Networking

iTunes (Apple), 119–121

J

Job responsibilities

of current job, 113–117, 125

planning for, 137–138

Jobs, Steve, 102

Job satisfaction, 11–21, 169–175

advantages of working while seeking employment, 101–105, 171–173

assessing current job and, 91–93

boss (managers) and, 13–15

co-workers and, 18–19

creating success by working, 170–171

enjoying work *versus* job, 173–174, 186

feeling overworked or undervalued, 17–18

internal politics and, 15–17

overview, 11–13, 169–170

prioritizing Career Plan for, 174–175

salary and, 19–20

Job skills. *See* Skills

Joyce, Amy, 56

L

Langley, Samuel Pierpont, 143–145

Lottery, fantasies about, 6–7

M

Management jobs, planning for, 138

Managers, dissatisfaction with, 13–15

Market segment, perfect job for, 96–99

Mastery-induced passion, 106

MBTI (personality test), 123

Meaning, finding, 59–61, 99

Moonlighting, 190

Motivation
  self-handicapping and making excuses, 49
  understanding, 143–147

N

Networking, 149–158
  benefits of, 151–152
  discussing career options with friends and contacts, 190–191
  expanding network, 156–158
  fear of, 155–156
  to learn about new career, 42, 190–191
  to overcome career boredom, 62

overview, 149–151
tips for, 152–155

O

O'Brien, William F., 213

Odeo, 119–121

Olympic Games (1996, Atlanta), 50–52

One-, Three-, and Five-Year Plan (Career Plan Step 4), 133–141, 147

Opiyo, Benard Didacus, 180–181

Organizational culture, career boredom and, 56–58

Overworked, feeling, 17–18

P

Part-time work, 190, 191, 197–198

Passion, 101–112
  changing aspects of current job, 110
  enticement of follow-your-passion jobs, 102–103
  identifying best aspects of current job, 105–107, 111
  identifying negotiable aspects of current job, 109–110, 112

Passion (*continued*)
  identifying worst aspects of
    current job, 108–109,
    111
  obstacles to
    follow-your-passion
    jobs, 103–105
  overview, 101–102
Pay scale, dissatisfaction with,
  19–20
Perception, 203–204
Performance reviews,
  analyzing, 129–130
Personality testing, 43,
  123
Philanthropy, 177–182,
  181–182
Pie-in-the-sky thinking,
  about goals, 95–96
Planning, 133–141
  compensation and,
    138–139, 193–199
  determining role and,
    137–138
  for difficulty (*See* Seven Life
    Tools to Get You
    Through Difficult
    Times)
  managing employees *versus*
    working individually,
    138
  overview, 133–136

  for self-employment *versus*
    company employment,
    136–137
  for training and education,
    139–141, 191
Politics, in workplace, 15–17
Power of Work, The (Career
  Plan Step 8), 169–175
Preparation, for advancing
  career, 99–100
Prioritization, being rich and,
  68–69. *See also* "Rich"
Promotion, seeking, 61–63
Prudential, 185

R
Rahe, Richard, 184
Rath, Tom, 42, 122
Rescue fantasy, 6–7
Return on Investment
  (Career Plan Step 9),
  177–182
"Rich," 65–76
  defining, 66–68
  feelings about, 69–71
  money and, 69, 72–74
    (*See also* Compensation)
  overview, 65–66
  time and, 69, 74–75
  values and, 68–69
"Right" time, waiting for,
  163–164
Risk, taking, 217–218

Ross, Laurian, 177
Ross, Percy, 177–178

S
Salary, dissatisfaction with, 19–20
Sam's Club, 19
Self-employment, planning for, 136–137
Self-handicapping, with excuses, 49
Self-marketing, 131–132
Self-pity, avoiding, 206
Seven Life Tools to Get You Through Difficult Times, 201–209
  Adjust Your Perception, 203–204
  Choose to Act and Not Be Acted Upon, 206–207
  Control Your Emotions, 204–205
  Don't Allow Self-Pity, 206
  Don't Compare, 205–206
  Focus on What You Can Control, 205
  Have Grace Under Pressure, 207–208
  overview, 201–203, 208–209
  taking action with, 213–216
Shyness, overcoming, 155–156

Skills
  assessment of, 62
  mastering, 130–131
  planning for, 139–141
  transferability of, 41, 83
Snagajob.com, 197
Social media, for networking, 42, 154, 191
State of the Global Workplace (Gallup), 12, 19
Stimulation, seeking, 58–59
Strength Finders 2.0, 122
Strengths, 119–126
  building, 123–125
  comparing job responsibilities and, 125
  defined, 121–122
  identifying, 122–123
  overview, 119–121
Strengths Test 2.0, 42
Strug, Kerri, 50–52
Stuck, feeling, 77–84
Success, sharing, 177–182
Supervising roles, planning for, 138

T
"Thanks a Million" (Ross), 178
Time, being rich and, 69, 74–75
"Toxic" work environment, 19

Training
   planning for, 139–141
   taking classes in new career
      area, 191
Try-before-you-buy scenario,
      183–192
   changing careers for wrong
      reasons, 186–188
   defined, 184–186
   overview, 183–184
   prospective careers and
      jobs, 189–192
   seeking information about
      new career, 40–41, 62,
      188–189
Twitter, 119–121

U
Undervalued, feeling, 17–18
University of West Florida, 55
Uradi (Kenya) Girls High
      School, 180–181

V
Values, 68–69. *See also* "Rich"
Vocation vacation, 189–190
Vodanovich, Stephen, 55

W
Washington Post, 56
Wealth. See "Rich"
"What Do I Value and What
      Matters the Most to
      Me? (list), 69, 72. *See
      also* "Rich"
What Is Your Job? (Career
      Plan Step 1), 113–117
What Makes You Awesome at
      Work? (Career Plan
      Step 3), 127–132
Work, job versus, 173–174,
      186. *See also* Job
      satisfaction
Wright, Orville, 144–145
Wright, Wilbur, 144–145

Y
Your Community (Career
      Plan Step 6), 149–158